T0389272

Ann Lieberman has been a teacher, worked with teachers and is an ardent advocate for teachers. This inspiring little book, Ann Lieberman's last, packs in 50 years of her magnificent life's work that has changed how researchers and policy-makers think about teaching and how teachers see themselves. Ann Lieberman is the teacher's scholar and the scholar's teacher – respectful, thoughtful, inspiring, and collaborative. If you ever were a teacher, are a teacher, want to be a teacher or be with teachers, this is absolutely the book for you from probably the greatest living legend in the field.

Andy Hargreaves, *Research Professor, Boston College, USA*

Few educators have the scope, the wisdom, the experience, and the commitment to teacher leadership of Ann Lieberman. In this volume, she invites readers in to decades of valuable perspective on elevating teachers' voices and enabling teacher leadership in multiple contexts. Ann is a mentors' mentor, a teachers' teacher, and her infectious enthusiasm for empowering educators shines through. In an era that leaves many teachers feeling beat-down and beaten-up, Lieberman is relentlessly upbeat, describing the joyful work that inspires teachers to be the leaders the profession desperately needs.

Desiree Pointer Mace, *Professor of Education and Director of Graduate Education Programs, Alverno College, USA*

Ann's personally revealing account of her professional journey charts the questions and challenges that have shaped her education career over more than 50 years. Lieberman's ideas and insights have broadly influenced our understanding about the social realities of teaching and moved policies aiming to develop teachers' knowledge about effective practice closer to the classroom. *Teaching, Learning and Living* explains how and why Ann's thinking evolved. This engaging book offers a matchless opportunity to enter the inner world of a great education leader.

Milbrey McLaughlin, *David Jacks Professor of Education and Public Policy, Emerita, Stanford University*

It's not often that we get to read a 50-year perspective on teaching, learning, and research from one of the pioneers of the idea that teachers are learners and knowers, not just the objects or recipients of somebody else's research. *Teaching, Learning and Living* reflects Ann Lieberman's life-long commitment to these ideas and provides a highly-readable tour of the major projects that have animated a half century of work with teachers as leaders and research partners.

Marilyn Cochran-Smith, *Cawthorne Professor, Lynch School of Education, Boston College, USA*

In this book, Ann Lieberman provides an extraordinary window into the life of an extraordinary educator. Her early formation and the people and experiences that have touched and influenced her over the past five decades all come alive in these pages. Here, Ann does what she does best; she teaches us. And she teaches us not only about teaching, learning, and school reform; she teaches us about what matters most in education. Most importantly, she teaches us what it means to live a life of integrity, commitment, and value.

Lynne Miller, *Emerita Professor, University of Southern Maine, USA*

TEACHING, LEARNING AND LIVING

By tracing the development of Ann Lieberman's commitment to exploring the complex, entwined nature of teaching, learning and living, this book reflects on how research in teacher leadership and development has progressed and changed over the last fifty years.

This personal account highlights Lieberman's learning as she engaged in research to build collaborative ways of working. Portraying the fight for teacher participation in research studies about teaching, schooling and teacher improvement so that the complexity of their lives would be represented, and writing about the consideration of teachers' work in any efforts for school improvement, the book discusses the initial collaboration between researchers and teachers. It then proceeds to outline a number of research projects that document the changing relationship of research and teaching and offers guidance on some of the most important and successful programs and strategies in the field. It questions issues such as how to create a culture in the school that is supportive of teachers, and how research can best assist teachers to improve their work.

Teaching, Learning and Living is a personal, historical and professional look at the growth in knowledge that began to change the views of research and teaching and is a must-read for anyone interested in the development of teacher education.

Ann Lieberman is a Senior Scholar at the Stanford Center for Opportunity Policy (SCOPE) in Education at Stanford University, USA, and an Emerita Professor at Teachers College, Columbia University, USA.

TEACHING, LEARNING AND LIVING

Joining Practice and Research

Ann Lieberman

Routledge
Taylor & Francis Group

LONDON AND NEW YORK

First published 2018
by Routledge
2 Park Square, Milton Park, Abingdon, Oxon OX14 4RN

and by Routledge
711 Third Avenue, New York, NY 10017

Routledge is an imprint of the Taylor & Francis Group, an informa business

British Library Cataloguing-in-Publication Data
A catalogue record for this book is available from the British Library

Library of Congress Cataloging-in-Publication Data
Names: Lieberman, Ann, author.
Title: Teaching, learning and living : joining practice and research /
    Ann Lieberman.
Description: Abingdon, Oxon ; New York, NY : Routledge, 2018. |
    Includes bibliographical references.
Identifiers: LCCN 2017050159 | ISBN 9781138060364 (hbk) |
    ISBN 9781138060388 (pbk) | ISBN 9781315163109 (ebk)
Subjects: LCSH: Action research in education. | Teachers—In-service
    training. | Teachers—Professional relationships. | Educational leadership.
Classification: LCC LB1028.24 .L54 2018 | DDC 370.72—dc23
LC record available at https://lccn.loc.gov/2017050159

ISBN: 978-1-138-06036-4 (hbk)
ISBN: 978-1-138-06038-8 (pbk)
ISBN: 978-1-315-16310-9 (ebk)

Typeset in Bembo
by Apex CoVantage, LLC

CONTENTS

ANN LIEBERMAN BIOGRAPHY

Ann Lieberman is currently a Senior Scholar at the Stanford Center for Opportunity Policy (SCOPE) in Education at Stanford University. She is an Emerita Professor at Teachers College, Columbia University.

She was a Senior Scholar at the Carnegie Foundation for the Advancement of Teaching, where she co-directed the k-12 program with Tom Hatch. She has written or edited sixteen books including: *Teachers: Transforming Their World and Their Work*; *Building a Professional Culture in Schools*; *How Teachers Become Leaders*; as well as *Inside the National Writing Project* and *The Work of Restructuring Schools*.

Lieberman has served on numerous national and international advisory boards, including those of the United Federation of Teachers and the National Education Association. She is also a past president of the American Educational Research Association (AERA).

She is widely known for her work in the areas of teacher development and leadership, collaborative research, networks and school-university partnerships as well as the problems and prospects for understanding educational change. Her research career has continuously been about understanding the dynamics of changing practice, structure and the school culture, with teachers playing a major role as learners and leaders in the process.

PREVIOUS PUBLICATIONS BY ANN LIEBERMAN

Teacher Learning and Leadership: Of, By, and For Teachers
Ann Lieberman, Carol Campbell and Anna Yashkina
Abingdon: Routledge, 2017

Teacher Education Around the World
Edited by Linda Darling-Hammond and Ann Lieberman
Abingdon: Routledge, 2012

Mentoring Teachers: Navigating the Real-World Tensions
Ann Lieberman, Susan Hanson and Janet Gless
San Francisco: Jossey-Bass, 2012

How Teachers Become Leaders: Learning from Practice and Research
Ann Lieberman and Linda D. Friedrich
New York: Teachers College Press, 2010

Second International Handbook of Educational Change
Edited by Andy Hargreaves, Ann Lieberman, Michael Fullan and
David Hopkins
Dordrecht: Springer, 2009

Teachers in Professional Communities: Improving Teacher and Learning
Edited by Ann Lieberman and Lynne Miller
New York: Teachers College Press, 2008

*The Roots of Educational Change: International Handbook of
Educational Change*
Edited by Ann Lieberman
Dordrecht: Springer, 2005

Teacher Leadership
Ann Lieberman
San Francisco: Jossey-Bass, 2004

*Inside the National Writing Project: Connecting Network
Learning and Classroom Teaching*
Ann Lieberman and Diane R. Wood
New York: Teachers College Press, 2002

*Teachers Caught in the Action: Professional Development
that Matters*
Edited by Lynne Miller and Ann Lieberman
New York: Teachers College Press, 2001

Teachers – Transforming Their World and Their Work
Ann Lieberman and Lynne Miller
New York: Teachers College Press, 1999

*The Work of Restructuring Schools: Building from the
Ground Up*
Edited by Ann Lieberman
New York: Teachers College Press, 1995

*Teachers – Their World and Their Work: Implications for School
Improvement*
Ann Lieberman and Lynne Miller
New York: Teachers College Press, 1992

*Schools as Collaborative Cultures: Creating the
Future Now*
Ann Lieberman
New York: Falmer Press, 1990

Building a Professional Culture in Schools
Edited by Ann Lieberman
New York: Teachers College Press, 1988

Rethinking School Improvement: Research, Craft and Concept
Edited by Ann Lieberman
New York: Teachers College Press, 1986

Policy Making in Education, **82nd Yearbook of the National Society of Education (NSSE)**
Edited by Ann Lieberman and Milbrey W. McLaughlin
Chicago: University of Chicago Press, 1982

Time to Learn
Edited by Ann Lieberman and Carolyn Denham
Washington, D.C.: National Institute of Education, 1980

Staff Development: New Demands, New Realities: New Perspectives
Edited by Ann Lieberman and Lynne Miller
New York: Teachers College Press, 1979

1

A TEACHING LIFE

I was thirty-one, had three daughters (aged three, seven and nine) and a loving husband, and was ready to go for my first teaching job. We were living in Los Angeles but there were no jobs there, so I went to Simi Valley, a new and fast-growing suburb, but which was thirty miles from home. I got a job as a sixth grade teacher and found that I had forty-five kids in my class in my first year of teaching. Although it was over fifty years ago, sometimes it feels like yesterday.

I had gone to UCLA and was fortunate to have one of the last of the John Dewey followers as my teacher. You were supposed to engage the students in learning, find out what they knew by creating an environment where they were being presented with a lot of information, some of which they knew and some of which was to be found out. Our college preparation was that we were to DO everything we were going to teach. If you were going to take a class field trip, you needed to take it yourself and write about it. If you were going to have students write about something, you needed to take the challenge and write something yourself. In this way we were to learn what we were going to teach, understanding its nuances through our own experience!

We ended up having a box full of ideas that we were actively involved in creating; we all called it "The Box Course". The Box stayed in the closet and I worked hard to figure out how to involve the students in a variety of subjects, some that I loved (Social Studies, Literature, P.E.) and some that I needed to learn more about (Science, Math and more). But it was complicated. How do you handle the two kids who were brilliant, the seven boys who couldn't read, and all the rest who were sometimes eager, sometimes bored, sometimes highly engaged, sometimes somewhere else in their mind and body?

Our principal was always showing us the latest research on teaching. No one talked about what we knew as teachers, nor what we experienced in our classrooms. There was always a lot of information about "what research says". Some of us were actually curious about the research, but it failed to hold our sustained interest as it never included the complexities of our teaching lives and the daily nature of our work. It seemed more like an interesting set of abstractions! Somehow most of us couldn't figure out how to make these abstractions connect to our work in our classrooms.

I think some of my best education about teaching took place there in the classroom. How do you involve this huge array of learners? How do you switch from subject to subject? How do you organize a whole day so that you have greater periods of intensity, time to relax, sometimes heavily involve students, group kids differently, deal honestly and openly with a full curriculum and keep the momentum going? How do you deal with students who are totally disconnected from what you are hoping to do with them? Us newbies had no one to talk to. Although Ms. Evans came once a month to DO staff development with us, it had nothing to do with the context of our classrooms or the culture of our school, and it seemed like a lot of ideas unrelated to our teaching lives. She would bring all kinds of ideas for classroom use, but somehow what she brought seemed to have no connections with what we were experiencing as teachers in our particular contexts. The ideas were interesting, but none of us could figure out how to use the ideas, learn about them over time, and somehow get supported in the process.

Living the complexity of a classroom

It was here that my angst began! Those of us in the classroom were learning all kinds of things every day in our classrooms, but nobody seemed interested at that time. We were learning about the incredible differences among our students, what worked, what failed, and what seemed unrelated to our students' lives and understandings.

For openers, many of the girls were clearly in their adolescence, while most of the boys seemed so much younger and not quite there yet. The normal three groups that you would organize in a regular-sized class (thirty students or fewer) didn't work in my class. The seven male non-readers were a special group and clearly needed special help. (We did not have anyone else in the school to help.) How to think about the momentum of this big class was huge – not only how to engage students wherever possible, but actually to find room for them in this regular-sized classroom. It was up to us as individual teachers to figure all this out by ourselves. I wondered if there was a different way or someone to help us learn strategies for use in our classrooms! Was teaching always like this? Take a curriculum and somehow figure out how students could learn it?

Talking it over at home and figuring it out!

The way I solved my need for help was to talk with my husband about three or four kids – **Every Night**. Like most teachers, I was good at telling stories about the kids, but knew nothing about getting to the point, picking out salient characteristics, always talking too much . . . Finally, my patient husband said to me one night, "Can't you just give me an outline? Tell me one big idea about a kid, shorten your descriptions . . ." I needed to learn how to do that. But it took time. I was concentrating on how to keep a certain momentum in the classroom, otherwise I would lose them, and giving up on details seemed hard.

I figured out that I could put the class schedule on the blackboard. I did that and had no idea whether the kids ever read it, but it helped me think about TIME and how to move from subject or strategy so I could organize my time for the day. Of course, things went over the time allotted, or someone would interrupt the class, or things could get really involved, but it was a crutch that I used for at least the first six months of the term. And somehow it helped me move to another strategy when the students were almost finished, to think quickly about how to change the tempo of the involvement of students when it seemed necessary, and, in general, to keep me mostly on the road to keeping track of the kids, the assignments, the noise, the involvement, the subject matter, and the time everything took.

The car pool: Sharing our work!

Since I lived thirty miles from our school, I was fortunate to find two other teachers at my school who lived fairly close to me. We created a car pool so that all of us would not have to drive sixty miles a day alone over two mountain ranges. There were no freeways in Los Angeles at the time, and to get to our school you had to go over two mountain ranges before you got to Simi Valley from the San Fernando Valley. But our car pool turned out to be a glorious ride! We talked about our class, the kids who were hard to reach, the things we tried that somehow worked, where we tried something and it bombed, and ideas we had for faculty meetings, for lunch, for our principal, for just connecting teachers to each other. We talked loudly, fast, furiously and in a fun-loving manner. We all looked forward to driving to school and I volunteered to talk with our principal about our ideas. He was a really nice guy, but new to the job and was trying to be a "good principal". We were both the same age and both had kids. He and I had a very good rapport. (He had a book that gave directions for what to say and how to behave as a new principal.)

I think he liked our ideas, but never really used any of them. He too was trying to figure out how to get through the day, so our ideas – even if he thought they were good – interrupted how he was learning to do his job. He was stuck on playing tapes of lectures during lunch. And we were just trying to eat our lunch and relax for twenty minutes. We all wondered why the joy we felt coming to school couldn't ever be replicated. When we arrived at school, we were met with silence and struggle without the comradeship that we felt in the car. .

Teaching and research: Were they in conflict?

One thing that seemed certain to me was that without the teachers' involvement in helping to think through what needed changing or improving, there would be few, if any, changes or improvements in our classroom work! Research, we were beginning to learn, was for people in the university who picked things to study from the outside. They needed to study lots of teachers and principals because numbers were all that counted in those days. Getting close to a teacher, finding out how they think and work, we reasoned, could never happen. This was to become a passion in my career and professional life. I didn't know how to do it, didn't really know how to even think about how teachers could be involved, but I was passionate and positive that without our involvement no one would ever get the whole story – the *inside* view and *our* questions – as well as the outsider's view and theirs.

After school: Outside *researcher needs* the inside view!

One day, our principal called us all to the office after school and introduced us to a woman who was doing research on elementary principals. She wanted us to fill out a questionnaire that seemed to be about *our* principal, his role, behavior, and effects on us. I zipped through the questionnaire very quickly and went up to talk with her. I asked her what she was doing and why this paper with all these questions about the principal was important to her. Her answers fascinated me! She said she was doing research for her dissertation and it was about the role of the principal in elementary schools. Further, she said she needed to have at least fifteen schools (and principals) so that she could find some common themes. Principals were "key actors" in the elementary school, she said, and she wanted to find out the obvious and subtle reasons why this was so. Needless to say, I was intrigued. She was asking us to talk about the principal and his effects on us! That was an amazing idea to me. I knew nothing about research, but had plenty to say about our principal. The idea that you could frame that kind of idea and go and ask teachers for their views really got to me. Maybe *research* could be framed with teachers' as well as researchers' questions? Maybe we could design a way of talking about our teaching lives and our students? Maybe we could describe the realities of teaching, student learning, and how they are connected? Maybe we could describe the hundreds of decisions you make, the dynamics of classroom life, and how you struggle to meet the learning as well as emotional needs of your students?

Learning by doing: The Volcano Project

Although I knew little about the arts and how to involve students in doing something artistic, one day while reading about volcanoes and how they grow and change, I decided we could actually make a volcano in our classroom. To me, this seemed like an important idea that might make the material about volcanoes much more interesting for the kids. I read that you needed chicken wire to create some kind of a cone, which you could attach to a piece of wood and shape it so that it looked similar to the shape of a volcano. Then I had the kids tear newspaper into pieces and soak the pieces in paste until the chicken wire was fully covered with the newspaper. I did know how to make papier mâché. We then left it for a few days while the paste dried. Several days later, a group of students painted it red and brown to simulate what they thought a volcano would look like on the outside. There was a small opening at the front, so I thought – since the kids had done so much work – that we could put a small candle inside which would draw attention to this incredible thing that they had built. Little did I know that when the paste got warm it would start to drip down the sides – the students stood up and yelled, "Look, the volcano is erupting!" Sure enough, as the paste, warmed by the candlelight all around the volcano, was dripping down the sides. It looked very real to all of us! We were all stunned and for well over an hour we all stared at this tremendous monument of a volcano that was "erupting". I don't know what the kids learned, but I realized that learning could be greatly enhanced by students engaging in serious "hands-on" projects along with their reading and studying. I was to learn again and again how many different ways students could be "involved" in learning, not just passively listening or even reading what others have to say. Again, it showed me how exciting it was for the students to be involved in creating something and how it could then lead to wanting to know more (and do more).

Although that first year was long ago, it left an indelible imprint on me. It taught me so much about what it meant to really engage students and how much more complicated it was to be a teacher. No one ever taught us to make connections between what the kids were "doing" and how they could ask questions of their reading and figure out what was worth writing. Those kinds of connections did not come naturally and took time to really understand by experiencing them in a variety of different ways.

Although involving students in our teacher education program to learn about teaching was about "doing" things, making things, engaging in figuring out how students could be physically as well as intellectually involved, it didn't really *take* until it happened in my classroom. How could us "insiders" somehow develop a voice? Teach people how complicated teaching is? Get people outside schools to recognize that school cultures and teachers in classrooms are anything but simple? That learning to control the momentum was a critical part of keeping students involved . . . that sometimes the best of plans do not work, while other times you try things and they take off? The Volcano Project was an important part of my learning to understand why experience was important and how it could lead to intellectual work, reading, studying, and deepening students' learning.

A tough lesson: Learning to deal with problem students

Perhaps one of the biggest lessons I learned in teaching that first year was that sometimes doing the obvious doesn't work with problem students, so you have to be lucky too. I was very involved with having students write stories, poems, or basically anything that interested them. So I set about engaging students in how they could write (about their favorite character or friend – a made-up character – a family member, an event, a story etc.)

One of the biggest problem students I had was a boy who would deliberately drop his book about ten times a day, I assumed to get attention. I tried all kinds of pleas, ideas, little punishments, etc. but nothing would work. Given the opportunity to write, Carl wrote about a Martian Man. I told the class that the best story would also get music and lyrics written by my husband (who was a songwriter and lyricist). Carl's story was actually very interesting and I chose him. My husband wrote music and lyrics to his story. And, to my thrilling surprise Carl was so excited that he stopped dropping books and became a very involved student. At Open House he showed his parents his story and the song that went with it, and took them all around the room showing them all kinds of things that our class did. He became a model student! How do you explain these kinds of things to an outsider? All I knew was that the classroom was an incredibly complicated place – incredibly different kinds of students with different learning styles, huge differences between boys and girls in the sixth grade, many subjects to teach, figuring out how to engage students in a variety of subjects and strategies – and somehow keeping up the interest of forty-five kids! So far, I was lucky! I hit a home run in physical education, facilitated a volcano eruption, and got Carl to stop dropping his book and join the class.

Learning to deal with the complexity

I was learning slowly that teaching was a constant struggle. You are always trying to connect to your students in ways that encourage and support their interest, excitement, engagement and learning. And, it was clear to me that you had to learn that sometimes you could be exhilarated, often exhausted, and always struggling to put it all together. It was getting better, but it still reminded me of knitting somehow. Sometimes you were so satisfied with the results. Other times you tried something and it really didn't work, while other times you experimented, it worked and was even better than you expected. It was not an exact science, but rather working with many human beings was almost always messy. So I learned to get used to it. I was always trying to make it all come together, but realized that sometimes it wasn't going to happen.

I learned from our car pool that there might be ways we could learn, not only in the car coming to school, but that school itself could be a place where we talked, learned together and supported each other. But how? How was this to happen? Who would do it? What would it take to replicate the connection we felt toward each other? Could we ever break the isolation that we all felt when the bell rang to begin class?

Expanding our knowledge

Waller (1932) put forth the idea that teachers should be involved and it struck me that this was the kind of work that I wanted to do. His words really spoke to me when he said:

> *It is not possible to develop the personalities of students favorably without giving like opportunities to teachers, and it is not possible to liberate students without liberating teachers.*

I first read George Homan's book (1950) very early in my educational career and was incredibly impressed with the idea that you could think about teaching and your relationship with other teachers in a very different way. He talked about activities (what you do), interactions (relationships you have with others) and sentiments (one's feelings about the group). I immediately began to translate this into how I thought about my colleagues, what we did, and how I felt about them. It was the first time that I realized that academics were busy conceptualizing how people thought, worked and related to each other. And that gave me a way of thinking about my school, the teacher next door, my friends in the car pool, and my relationship to all of this.

Perhaps the biggest and most important contribution to our understanding of schools and how to improve them came with Seymour Sarason's book entitled: *The Culture of the School and the Problem of Change* (Sarason, 1972). He was the first person to actually describe a school as a culture with its rituals, rules etc. and to link the "culture" to the problem of trying to change or improve education in classrooms. For those living in one of the cultures it was clear that there were ways of doing things, and the idea of changing or improving anything was a far distant idea. But, in some ways, it gave credibility to a small, but growing, group of researchers who were now thinking about and writing about the process of change in schools (Granovetter, 1973; Lortie, 1975; Parker, 1977). Each, in their way, were trying to get at the complexity of teaching and how to improve it. Some were suggesting the organization of loose networks, while others were trying to get at what teaching appeared to be – from the inside.

In England, there was a growing movement around the idea of "action research". Teachers could pose a question and engage in actively collecting data (from the inside) and learning from it – suggesting that teachers' questions and answers were a way of getting at the complexities of classrooms (Stenhouse, 1975). This was a beginning realization that to improve practice, teachers would have to be serious partners in the process. Although this seemed obvious, it wasn't to most people. This idea spoke to the role of teachers in the 1960s, where there was an operating assumption that outsiders needed to tell teachers how to improve. The idea that teachers could study their own practice was new and refreshing, even though it was mostly in the books!

References

Granovetter, M.S. (1973) The strength of weak ties. *American Journal of Sociology*, 78(6), 1360–1380.

Homans, G.C. (1950) *The Human Group*. New York: Harcourt, Brace and Company.

Lortie, D. (1975) *Schoolteacher: A Sociological Study of Teaching*. Chicago, IL: University of Chicago Press.

Parker, A. (1977) *Networks for Innovation and Problem Solving and Their Use for Improving Education*. Unpublished manuscript. Washington, D.C: National Institute of Education, School Capacity for Problem Solving.

Sarason, S. (1972) *The Culture of the School and the Problem of Change*. Boston: Allyn & Bacon.

Stenhouse, L. (1975) *An Introduction to Curriculum Research and Development*. London: Heinemann.

Waller, W. (1932) *The Sociology of Teaching*. New York: Wiley & Sons.

2

TEACHERS AS PARTNERS

Not objects of research

Although I had a teaching credential, I did not have a Masters degree. So, when my husband was hired to write five songs for a movie, he said, "Why don't you go for your Masters degree? We can now afford it". So I took a year off from teaching and studied for a degree. While there, I became very involved in reading, thinking about schools, classroom life, etc. And several of my professors suggested that I get a doctorate. I had no idea what that would allow you to do, but it did seem like people with doctorates did many things at the same time – they taught, did research, wrote books and articles, went to all kinds of meetings, gave speeches – and some of them even traveled to other countries. All of this had great appeal to me as I liked doing a lot of things in my work and personal life. By this time, I was finally beginning to appreciate how much I needed to learn. The passion to involve teachers was strong, but the intellectual ideas needed plenty of development.

Becoming an activist student in a School Improvement Project

I decided to study for a doctorate at UCLA and lucked out. I got into a program run by John Goodlad, who was just about to become Dean at UCLA. He was a well-known educational expert (even though I had never heard of him when I was a teacher). His idea at the time was to create a consortium of schools to encourage and support school improvement. He called the program *The League of Cooperating Schools*. (There were eighteen elementary schools in Southern California as part of the Institute for the Development of Educational Activity [I/D/E/A]). In the process of being in a group, Goodlad's idea was that principals were the "key agents of reform". The group would serve as both an educational connection for all the principals and a means of support, and in the process we would all learn about the process of change and how to support improvement in schools. There were twelve men and me as doctoral students. (That will tell you something about the role of women in education at the time).

Working in our schools: Learning about change

Our primary assignment as doctoral students in the *League* was to learn from our experiences with our schools. Each of the doctoral students were assigned two schools where we were responsible for somehow getting the conversation of improvement going and hopefully encouraging ideas and discussion, and hopefully action among the teachers and their principal. One of the big ideas of the *League* was that the principal was to facilitate improvement among the teachers as he/she was the "key agent of change". We were learning how to get teachers to talk with one another, while the principal was learning to facilitate the conversation. While we all went to our schools, made friends and learned how to bring in articles, create discussion groups, and sometimes find teachers who wanted to try new things, others wondered why we were there. But the principals were excited about being the center of attention. The research study for the program was called SECSI (The Study of Educational Change and School Improvement). The principals' group was almost all male; there was one woman in the group. The group met regularly to discuss the growing themes of the process of change, individualizing instruction and involving teachers in improving their teaching. A small research team was going to track the conversation and the process of change as it happened in the schools. There was a sense that men dominated the intellectual ideas about education and the women did the teaching. Stereotypes (at this time) were right out there. Some of the principals had no problem describing "helping the girls" in their schools or "guiding the girls as they drove on the freeway". It seemed an accepted fact that somehow men were in charge, while women worked hard at teaching and needed the men (as principals) to guide them.

Inequality for men and women: An accepted practice

On a personal level, I found out that I was making $1,000 less than the men as a doctoral student. We were all doing exactly the same thing: we all had the responsibility to make something happen in our two schools. I went to the person in charge of the money to find out why this was so. He actually looked at me and said "You have a husband" before getting up and leaving the room. The men were making $3500 a year, and I was making $2500. It was not about the money as much as the fairness of us all getting the same remuneration for the same responsibilities! This kind of inequity was accepted practice and there was literally nowhere to go to bring up the inequities and change this practice.

Learning to facilitate discussion and action in my schools

My two schools were entirely different in their feel, culture and leadership. One of my schools was in Culver City, California (not too far from UCLA). The principal was in a doctoral program at UCLA so he tried to practice some of the things he was learning in his classes. The other school was in Corona, which was over 30 miles from my home and definitely more rural in feel and scope. The principal was well liked, but very quiet and undemanding. He encouraged me to take over the discussion of "individualized instruction", which was one of the hot ideas being discussed at that time. When I came to the school, the teachers all thought I was an expert. After all, they figured I had driven thirty miles to get there and came every other week. It seemed like I was now an *outsider* to the teachers. And to some, I was also a researcher. My own view was that I was learning to look at a whole-school culture and trying to understand, from the outside, how to engage teachers in discussion about teaching, learning and individualized instruction, and how they might think about what it would look like in their classroom from the inside. I was a teacher now assuming a new role as an organizer of professional development in two different schools, trying to understand how to create conversation and ownership of improvement of practice as a collective ideal. It was an extraordinary way to learn about the school culture (and how to change it), and, at the same time, to understand the role of the principal as he or she related to the teachers.

The role of the change agent

From my perspective, I was a learner, trying to create structures for discussion with teachers, where they were not only involved but were the primary actors and movers in the school. Our discussions started with the **What** questions? – What is individualized instruction? What is its importance? What would help to get the discussion going? And pretty quickly we got to the **How** questions – How do you organize a group of students? How do you make assignments where students can adhere closely to their learning patterns? (What kind of materials do you use?) How do you organize a whole class doing individualized instruction? (What is the role of the teacher in individualized classrooms?) **Where** do you start?

It took time, but in about three months, the teachers in both schools were beginning to talk, ask questions, figure out how they might try to individualize instruction, and figure out what they needed to know and do to make it happen. In both schools, the teachers seemed to be enjoying their newfound relationships with their colleagues, and I enjoyed working with them to learn how to organize and structure conversations that the teachers felt were worth having. I was still a teacher, but now I was several steps removed from the day-to-day work. We were enjoying the new friendships that we were all making as a part of the consortium. I was learning to engage teachers in discussion, bring materials that enhanced the discussion, and involve them in both leading and engaging in expanding their work and their understanding of "individualized instruction".

City and country: Different school cultures

The principals were both radically different. The Culver City principal was going to UCLA for his doctorate (like me) and he used the new vocabulary that he was learning in the university program (**facilitation, organizing the school culture, building leadership** among the teachers, **being a change agent, supporting change**. . .). But I was to learn that they had not yet learned that principals come with a lot of power in the role and that they need to develop leadership and participation among the teachers. But the teachers were becoming more open and more ready to talk about and figure out what "individualized instruction" was and why it might be helpful for student learning.

Corona: More Rural and Friendly

The Corona school was more rural and friendly, and was very different in its culture and connections to the principal. He was very gentle, kind and quiet. He did not see himself in any way as a change agent (which was one of the new expressions of the day). He simply relinquished all leadership and organizing to me! I came and brought articles to read, which we then discussed. Teachers began to talk more readily about their students, and what worked and what didn't. And they began to say that they looked forward to my coming as it got the teachers talking together, clearly breaking the isolation of the classroom.

I was learning how to engage teachers, how to use outside ideas to connect to inside work, and how to create a sense of community of effort – where one had not existed before. We were becoming "educational friends" and "colleagues" in a search for understanding the latest ideas for supporting student learning and engagement together.

Building relationships/doing research: Role conflict ensues

We had two separate groups working in *The League of Cooperating Schools*. One group (all of us students working on getting our doctorate) were working with the schools, trying to get conversation going, bringing in materials to discuss and helping facilitate a collaborative discussion with the teachers and their principals. We talked among ourselves, sharing what we were learning with each other. The other group (the researchers) were designing questions to be asked of the schools so that they could document the process of change and school improvement. They were clearly the research group. We went to the schools every other week and the researchers designed questions to ask the teachers and their principal as part of their research in their university offices. We were building relationships with the teachers and their principals. The research group was at the university figuring out what questions to ask, what research design they should use, and how they were going to collect the data.

Collecting quantitative data only

When I was not going to class or to one of my schools, I was a doctoral student with the other twelve men. The doctoral students were working with their schools, trying to help facilitate discussion on individualized instruction, and the research group was figuring out what questions to ask the teachers and how to obtain quantitative data for use in their research. It was the 1960s, and quantitative data was all that was recognized by the research community as legitimate. This meant that they were going to have to collect enough data to be able to say something about the processes of change and the changing organizational and instructional work, and what the teachers and principals were doing and hopefully learning. And they needed to show all this with enough numbers since that was all that mattered to the research community. Unfortunately, the students working with the schools and the researchers did not work together, nor did they know what the research was all about. We were two separate groups, each doing a different job!

Insiders and outsiders: Objects or partners

The first conflict came when the research group asked me to report on the research and to pause every few minutes so that they could document the teachers' responses. I objected to this mechanistic way of giving them the research data, especially since I had worked so hard to make friends and create real discussion while we learned to work together. I was finally in a position where I could learn to structure discussion that mattered to teachers. They were involved and feeling good about their participation. Now the research group was asking me to pause every ten minutes as I reported the data to the teachers, so that they could get some additional responses to use as evidence. I saw this as an imposition on my friendship with the teachers and a strangely uncomfortable way of getting data. These were my colleagues! For a whole week, we talked, argued and tried to make the research group sensitive to the work that we had done. I was to learn, once again, that teachers were still objects to researchers and that they were NOT considered partners in the work.

It took many meetings to figure out how to collect data and not destroy the work that the students had been doing for months. We finally reached a compromise, but I was now more convinced than ever that we needed to find out how to make teachers true partners in research – not just objects of researchers' questions. The process of how we worked as a team has been written about by Bentzen et al. (1974), entitled *Changing Schools: The Magic Feather Principle*. Goodlad, as an experienced and well-known educator, expected that we would all learn together how to improve schools, how to initiate and sustain the process of change, and how to support principals as "key agents of change". We were all to find out how complicated this was and how none of us knew the answers, but how all of us learned over time together to listen to the different roles people held (teachers, principals, researchers, doctoral students), different perspectives on the work of school improvement, and the important nuances of the change processes in education.

The Magic Feather Principle

It was decided in the first year that we would help schools help themselves (hence the Magic Feather Principle). This became our first contribution (Bentzen et al., 1974). We would encourage the process of improvement, create strategies that seemed to work, and figure out together how to support the process. Our meetings were about what was happening in the schools, what things we had noticed and how receptive schools were to engaging in the process of improvement with our support. Through much discussion, we realized that we were engaging the school in *dialogue, decision-making, action, and evaluation*. DDAE became the mantra of our work together with the schools. We realized that we were inventing a process of change in our schools: getting teachers to talk (and read) about individualized instruction; eventually deciding that they would try to "individualize" instruction in their class (somehow); and that they would create some limited small group project where students would work on their individualized projects. After doing so, they would try to evaluate what they had learned, what the students had learned, and how to improve the process. This too ended up in a book entitled *Teachers on Individualization: The Way We Do It* (Shiman, Culver, and Lieberman, 1974), which includes chapters written by teachers about how they individualized instruction in their classrooms. And we realized that we were discovering many different issues that had to do with changing the culture of schools and the roles and relationships of the people in them (Culver and Hoban, 1973).

Inside the school culture: And outside in the research community

This was an incredible opportunity for me. I learned about how to work with schools in a way that engaged them in powerfully participating with others to improve their schools. But I also learned that the research that we were doing was too narrow and too restricted to gathering numbers, rather than also gathering the perspectives of the school people themselves – particularly the teachers. What the project exposed to all of us was that we all knew little about the complexities of change, and that in order for change to happen, the people who needed changing were not just the teachers but the research community as well. To depend on outsiders for collecting quantitative data without the participation of the teachers and principals (and their view of change) was to leave out important parts of the program and what the change processes actually were and how they were enacted. This was to come in later years, but at least our publications tried to get at the whole picture. For me personally, I learned that to achieve collaboration and an understanding of the complexities of changing school cultures, we needed to collaborate fully with the school people. Both principals and teachers needed to be a part of the research as partners, not objects. This was to become my lifelong passion, and being an active participant taught me that there was much work to be done in the future. Working *with* schools, not *on them* was so graphically displayed in this program that it was hard not to see how research had to change, as well as our roles in it. I was lucky that I was to get a position at Teachers College, where many before me had fought for these very same issues.

Expanding our knowledge

> *We have come to understand that teachers are professionals precisely because they operate under conditions of inherent novelty, uncertainty and chance.*
>
> (Shulman, 1999)

> *Policies are normally defined for general circumstances, typically devoid of nuance or conditionality. Practice, on the other hand, is terrifyingly local and specific.*
>
> (Shulman, 1999)

What we were experiencing was to be written about many years later, but we tried to document as much as possible what the *League* and our roles in it seemed to be bringing about. This was clearly a landmark project!

In the first book by Bentzen and associates (1974), *Changing Schools: The Magic Feather Principle*, we were trying to understand the processes of change as we saw them. We realized that the *League* was a new social system for the principals and that we could actually look at changes in how the principals acted over the five years of the program. There were case studies, field notes, and what change looked like from our perspective.

Those of us working with teachers kept field notes and did case studies of actual schools (and the teachers in them). But the power of the book entitled *Teachers on Individualization* (1974) was that it was actually written by the teachers who were individualizing instruction in their schools and felt confident enough to write about their classroom. We edited the book, but the teachers wrote the cases.

The last book we wrote was entitled *The Power to Change: Issues for the Innovative Educator* (1974). The book turned out to be an important collection of the many issues we discovered over the course of the five years, written by different people who had confronted and worked on different issues as we tried to document the program over the five years. Some chapters were concerned with the power of the principal, learning to work together, learning to problem solve, to name a few.

These three books are predecessors of a massive literature on change in schools which was to come.

References

Bentzen, M.B. and associates (1974) *Changing Schools: The Magic Feather Principle.* A Charles F. Kettering Foundation Program. New York: McGraw-Hill Book Company.

Culver, C. & Hoban, G. (1973) *The Power to Change: Issues for the Innovative Educator.* A Charles F. Kettering Foundation Program. New York: McGraw-Hill Book Company.

Shiman, D., Culver, C., & Lieberman, A. (1974) *Teachers on Individualization: The Way We Do It.* A Charles F. Kettering Foundation Program. New York: McGraw-Hill Book Company.

Shulman, L. (1999) Foreword. In: Darling-Hammond, L. & Sykes, G. (Eds.) *Teaching as the Learning Profession: Handbook of Policy and Practice.* San Francisco: Jossey-Bass, pp. xiii–xiv.

3

TEACHERS: THEIR WORLD AND THEIR WORK

I had been at Teachers College for several years and was still totally convinced of the idea that researchers were trying to change education from the *outside* with simple solutions to complex processes that occur on the *inside* of classrooms.

I had made friends with Ron Brandt, who was then the editor of *Educational Leadership*, and he got me interested in the work of the Association for Supervision and Leadership Development (ASCD). I was excited to learn that they published books. Lynne Miller and I decided to write a convincing book about teachers' authentic work in both elementary and secondary schools. I had met Lynne at my first academic job at the University of Massachusetts and we became good friends – sharing many things together, including our views of research and teaching practice. And we were fortunate that Ron liked our work and decided to publish our first book written together, sponsored by ASCD. It was called *Teachers: Their World and Their Work*.

We were determined to write about what classrooms were like. Beyond our experience, we also wanted to try to conceptualize why classrooms were so complex. We hoped that this would provide the evidence for our view that teachers must be included somehow with researchers if school improvement was the goal. We needed to show (rather than tell) what we and others were beginning to write about – that explained both practically and conceptually what the inside of classrooms really looked like in all its complexities.

Beginning conceptions of teaching

To start, we felt that we needed to provide a set of understandings about teaching that described the daily life of a teacher. These we called the **social realities of teaching**.

- Teachers need to learn a set of skills that are both cognitive and affective. How this happens becomes one's professional identity.
- The most important rewards for teachers come from students.
- The connections between teaching and learning are uncertain.
- The codification of the professional knowledge that a teacher needs is difficult to obtain because of the many contingencies in teaching.
- Because of conflicting goals for teaching, teachers must decide on a set of values that work for them (how are we supposed to teach subject matter content and socialize our students to learn to think? Ask questions? Make contributions? Develop learning skills? Make friends?)
- Lack of support and isolation best describes the teacher's classroom environment.
- Despite efforts to "scientize" teaching, it is very much an art learned in practice.

(Lieberman and Miller, 1984)

All of these understandings happen in the privacy of one's classroom. In a strange way, learning how to teach has everything to do with how you learn to manage both getting students to learn something and making friends with them, and somehow dealing with what is planned (and unplanned) and keeping the class momentum moving.

Class sizes vary from twenty to forty-five students (I had forty-five students). But despite the numbers, it is about how you try to build a positive culture with individuals and keep the group moving; how you plan, but come to realize that unplanned things happen along the way. For most teachers, their learning is in their particular classrooms and most of it is learned in isolation from other adults. How do you explain all this to your friends and family?

Powerful effects of isolation

Isolation does many things for teachers. On the positive side, you can try all kinds of things that might look strange to an outsider. You are free (in most cases) to design the way you work by yourself. And if you are open to learning, teaching is an incredible way to connect not only to your students' learning, but to your own. But, of course, there is also the negative side of isolation.

You often become very fixed in your ways of working and are not very open to others, their ideas, the research, books, and the outside world. This becomes more evident as others (those from the district, the principal, staff developers, etc.) come with ideas that they want you to try. Unfortunately, isolation teaches one to be wary of others' ideas and often very protective of your own.

The elementary classroom

> *Endemic uncertainties complicate the teaching craft and hamper the earning of psychic rewards. Intangibility and complexity impose a toll. . . it is most unlikely that so many teachers would experience difficulty if effective solutions were at hand.*
>
> *(Lortie, 1975, p. 159)*

I was fortunate to contact two of my friends who decided to team teach. They invited me to not only come and look at what they were doing, but to participate with them as well. This insider perspective over a short period of time gave me many more insights into what it was like to be an elementary school teacher. In just a few days of being in their classroom, I quickly learned a set of activities that began to set the norms of the classroom.

From the beginning, the teachers tried to find out what their students knew about reading and math. On Day 1 they asked the students to write something about themselves. The next day, 3×5 cards appeared on the bulletin board under the title ABOUT ME. Students had written comments like: "My brother left for college." "I suck my thumb, I'm skinny, and I love school." "I have one sister and my father died of a heart attack."

From Day 1, students got the sense that these teachers cared about them personally (as well as how they were as students). This kind of personalization seemed to be very important and meaningful to the students. By Day 2, teachers had already introduced particular activities and students were assigned to them (e.g. Reading 10:40, Joann, Ellen, Mark). As the week went by, different activities were on the board and students began to get a sense of the flow of activities. It only took a few days to realize that these teachers were moving from small groups, to individualized activities, to large group instruction as they went about the classroom helping move the flow and alternately being on and off the stage. Observing all this, it all seemed to flow easily from day to day. In conversation with the two teachers, I came to understand the various tensions that existed for them and how they seemed to face them as part of being a teacher and figuring out how to keep the flow going despite the hiccups.

The inevitable tensions of elementary teaching

Some of the inevitable tensions are:

1. How can you teach six to eight different subjects in the amount of time that you have during the day?
2. How do you group students accordingly and still maintain classroom interest and cohesion?
3. How do you keep track of the variety of activities and still maintain some sense of control?
4. How do you deal with the pressure of teaching the 3R's and somehow introduce other subjects, topics and ideas that occur and still have time for important ideas that arise?
5. How do you learn quickly how to make complicated ideas understandable to young children and still keep it exciting as you help translate the world for them?

I was to learn every day how good these teachers were and how quickly they adapted to their sixth grade students. It all looked so smooth.

> *The common sense understandings which teachers have of their problems bites deeper into reality than do the meanderings of most theorists. Teachers will do well to insist that any program of educational reform shall start with them, that it shall be based upon, and shall include their common sense insights.*
>
> *(Waller, 1967)*

Attempting to improve elementary teaching practice

All these things that we come to realize about elementary teaching and the tensions that arise in the process make engaging in improvement conditional on the social context of the school.

The social context of the school

Both national and local issues and concerns affect the school. These contexts affect how teachers feel, how they work, and what they are open to and ready for. If there is support for schools and teachers nationally (as in Finland and Canada), teachers are open to new ideas and feel excited about being a teacher. If there are continued criticisms and complaints about schools and teachers (both nationally and locally), teachers feel pressured, unloved, and sometimes feel negative about their work.

How schools and teachers are organized, how the local infrastructure is run, and how the school itself is managed has everything to do with the context of teaching and the treatment of teachers. The interpersonal relationships within a school are critical to how teachers feel about their work, their peers, the principal and their contributions as a teacher. These are all involved in the social context of teaching (Lieberman, 1969).

Life in secondary schools

Secondary schools differ from elementary schools in a number of different ways. To begin with, the secondary school is more complicated, more bureaucratic and much more difficult to negotiate. Although secondary teachers have similar tensions to those of elementary teachers, the bureaucratic nature of the organization suggests some common problems (or dilemmas). Because of its bureaucratic organization, teachers can close their door and have a great deal of autonomy, but they must also deal with the larger organization, its rules and regulations, its authority structure, its policies and procedures, and sometimes conflicting requirements. You have students for only an hour and you may have three to five different classes, unlike elementary classrooms that have the same teacher all day (and for a year). This alone causes a variety of stresses, tensions and differences.

The division of labor is far more complicated in secondary schools. You have a principal, assistant principals, department heads and teachers. It is commonly known that the most experienced teachers are often rewarded by the "best" classes. This alone causes a level of tension, anxiety and struggle among teachers.

There are also a number of positions in the school, such as guidance counselors, social workers, security guards, consultants – and these people often have their own authority in the school (often more than teaching faculty). One of the features of high schools is the fact that teachers often see 125–150 students each day and students arrive at their door from three to five periods every day. Most will admit that this arrangement makes it exhausting for teachers, despite other duties that are also part of their job. Teachers are also in charge of monitoring students' lateness and absences, and assume a variety of duties in the halls, lunchrooms, etc. Teachers must negotiate between "teaching" and helping maintain the social order of the school.

Unlike elementary teaching where the concern is how to keep the "day" moving and connected, secondary teachers must learn to put away the previous class and start with the students in front of them. Every teacher must deal with these concerns. For some, routine helps deal with the chaos that this causes.

For secondary teachers, they become subject specialists (Math, English or Physics). This, of course, makes teachers subject-matter focused (where elementary teachers are usually more child focused). Although secondary teachers view themselves as having a greater status than elementary teachers, they are often looked upon as being "special but shadowed" (Lortie, 1975).

Dealing with adolescence

Besides its bureaucratic nature, secondary schools must work with adolescents, which has never been easy. Parents and teachers can share many stories. For one thing, students have already had at least eight years in school and their academic fate has already been determined by others. Somehow, the secondary teacher must find a way to teach ALL students, regardless of their past. Some have clearly highly developed skills, while others are in need of basic skills, individual attention and motivation. I experienced these issues as a sixth grade teacher as well.

The faculty culture of secondary schools

Teachers must find a way to deal with the wide range of students they teach. They have to "cover" the material, somehow recognizing different degrees of difficulty for different students.

Teachers choose whether they will deal with personal issues that arise in their students, or choose to deal solely with the academic concerns of their subject matter. But besides dealing with adolescence, teachers in secondary school must figure out how they will deal with the faculty culture of the school. There are groups that form such as men, women, academic teachers, vocational teachers, and more. These groups form the culture for teachers. This is where they deal with adults, rather than students.

Elementary schools are primarily female, whereas the secondary culture is primarily male. Women often think of teaching as their life's work, whereas men often think about advancement and other positions in the educational hierarchy. The faculty group turns out to be important to teachers as it is the one that secondary teachers connect to in high school. Although the principal sets the tone, the group that one connects to is critical for even just an opportunity to relax and be with other adults.

Just this small discussion highlights the complexities of both elementary and secondary teachers and the fragility (dealing with the school and district context) on the one hand, and the strong connections on the other. Dealing with students is obviously the strong connection for elementary teachers; dealing with their subject matter, numbers of students, faculty connections and their participation in a bureaucracy describes the life and tensions of secondary teaching. Fortunately, a number of people in academia have taken as their life's work how to deal with the complexities of teaching.

Expanding our knowledge

In the 1980s and 1990s, several now well-known researchers dug deeply into the practices and problems of teaching, finally elevating the perspectives of teachers into the discussion. Perhaps one of the finest examples was Lampert's books, *How Do Teachers Manage to Teach: Perspectives on Problems in Practice* (1985) and *Teaching Problems and the Problems of Teaching* (2001). In both of these books, Lampert describes in incredible detail what it is like to teach, and what is meant by the complexity of teaching. In the latter book, as a university faculty member, she teaches a math class for a year, examining many of the things that teachers do and how each thing, in its own way, is *problematic*. She literally examines whole-class discussion, coverage of the curriculum, risk-taking, accomplishment, and more. Each is examined as a problem of teaching and as a research project. We get the practice and the conceptualization of teaching from the inside from a sensitive outsider who has helped develop a practitioner's perspective from a scholarly perspective.

Marilyn Cochran-Smith and Susan Lytle were among the earliest contributors to developing the understanding of teachers, their life and their work. They have helped change the view that teachers are only to be researched by others, by actually spearheading a move for teachers to do research in their own classrooms (Cochran-Smith and Lytle, 1993).

> *We argue that efforts to construct and codify a knowledge base for teaching have relied primarily on university-based research and ignored the significant contributions that teacher knowledge can make to both the academic research community and the community of school-based teachers.*
>
> *(Cochran-Smith and Lytle, p. 5)*

Their view that teaching can and should be learned both from outside researchers and those on the inside (teachers) is one of the most significant arguments that has helped change the traditional view of research on teaching.

Their influence was felt by many researchers interested in teachers and what they knew and practiced and how they could participate in the research community. Another important contribution was made by Freedman et al. (1999) as Sarah Freedman and her colleagues took on the investigation of teaching literacy in multicultural classrooms. Sarah Freedman and her colleague Elizabeth Simons created a teacher research network called *Multicultural Collaborative for Literacy and Secondary Schools* with teachers from four cities in the United States. Their goal was to bring together a diverse group of teachers representing both multiculturalism as well as working-class and middle-class teachers who would do research in their classrooms. The M-Class collaboration, as it became known, showed how teachers and university facilitators learned to work together and each redefine their roles. Teacher researchers moved toward important knowledge generation in teaching and learning, making collaboration with researchers and the organization of a network a significant contribution.

Over a ten-year period, Tom Hatch and I were responsible for creating a k-12 program on the Scholarship of Teaching at the Carnegie Foundation for the Advancement of Teaching. We were, from the beginning, interested in making teaching public to legitimate the role of teachers who were willing to examine their practice so that all of us could learn what was beneath the "complexities of teaching" and what it would mean if teaching could be a mode of scholarship. The CASTL Program (Carnegie Academy for the Scholarship of Teaching and Learning) provided an opportunity for several cohorts of teachers to come to Carnegie to inquire into their own teaching (Hatch et al., 2005). It was in the first cohort of teachers that they recognized the potential for using the web to share their teaching (see Yvonne Hutchinson and Sarah Capitelli, who are featured in Chapter 6 in this book). It was here that we all realized what you could tell people about your work and what you needed to show for deeper understanding (see www.insideteaching.org).

Involving teachers has become much more widely practiced as researchers and teachers have joined together in a variety of stances. Teacher research, new knowledge and scholarship have all occurred as a result of these partnerships. In the process, both teachers and researchers have learned to collaborate as well as shape new relationships, new learning and new possibilities.

References

Cochran-Smith, M. & Lytle, S. (1993) *Inside/Outside: Teacher Research and Knowledge*. New York: Teachers College Press.

Hatch, T., Ahmed, D., Lieberman, A., Faigenbaum, D., White, M.E., & Pointer-Mace, D. (2005) *Going Public with our Teaching: An Anthology of Practice*. New York: Teachers College Press.

Freedman, S., Simons, E., Kalnin, J., Casareno, A., & The M-Class Teams (1999) *Inside City Schools: Investigating Literacy in Multicultural Classrooms*. New York: Teachers College Press.

Lampert, M. (1985) How do teachers manage to teach: Perspectives on problems in practice. *Harvard Educational Review*, 55(2):178–194.

Lampert, M. (2001) *Teaching Problems and the Problems of Teaching*. New Haven, CT: Yale University Press.

Lieberman, A. (1969) "The Effects of Principal Leadership on Teacher Morale, Professionalism and Style in the Classroom." Doctoral Dissertation, University of California at Los Angeles.

Lieberman, A. & Miller, L. (1984) *Teachers: Their World and Their Work: Implications for School Improvement*. Washington, D.C: Association for Supervision and Curriculum Development.

Lortie, D. (1975) *Schoolteacher*. Chicago: University of Chicago Press.

Waller, W. (1967) *The Sociology of Teaching*. New York: John Wiley & Sons.

4

TEACHERS, STAFF DEVELOPERS, RESEARCHERS

Creating a collaborative team

I was a new professor at Teachers College and was excited by the fact that I could now figure out how to involve teachers *with* researchers and finally get some parity on the questions, the data and the explanations of what research could tell us about teaching and student learning with both outside and inside perspectives.

Gary Griffin, a colleague in the Curriculum and Teaching Department, and I were the heirs to the first study done by Betty Ward and Bill Tickunoff where the research was created by teacher teams working with a researcher. We reasoned that our study could expand the idea and have five teachers, a staff developer and a researcher, and that we could create several teams with this format in mind. This, we were sure, would provide a legitimate teacher voice. The funder was willing to support yet another study looking at different kinds of teams, what they studied, how they defined their research problem, how the data was collected and what they found out in the process. We were interested in having teachers express problems to be studied that emanated from their practice (that would include the complexities often left out) and how to collect information and talk about the findings. We felt that having more teachers would guarantee teacher knowledge and involvement in the process of doing the research. This seemed like a good match for us and the funders. We got the grant and were ready to work!

The three teams

We decided to help create three research teams that were not your standard fare. So we selected a team from the American Federation of Teachers (AFT), the teachers' union in New York City. They were beginning to talk about research, but we thought that here was an opportunity for them to be real players helping to create the research and be active participants, rather than just reading other people's work.

The second team was to be from the Board of Cooperative Services (BOCES). This group handled a variety of curricular needs for schools and represented teachers who taught a wide variety of students and subjects, including special education, and a variety of shared services for schools. As far as we knew, they were rarely involved in research and we thought this would be an interesting project for them to think not just about services for others, but about learning to frame some questions that they thought would be important to ask about their particular work with schools.

The third team was from Scarsdale, a district on Long Island, long known for its innovations and teacher involvement in improving their teaching. This school district had already advanced to having teachers become the staff developers in the district – those teachers who had already earned a reputation in a particular area of the curriculum. This was a decidedly strong district with respect and trust of teachers by the administration as well as the parent group. We thought this might make a huge difference in the questions they would ask and how they would go about being serious research partners, how they were involved (as teachers) and who might be involved on the team, where they could really represent the complexities of teachers' lives. For us, these three teams represented an interesting cross-section of education in New York City and its environs. There was the union that represented all teachers and their rights across urban and rural schools. There was an organization (BOCES) that represented a group that had many relationships and worked with a number of school districts throughout urban and suburban areas, and there was Scarsdale, an upper-middle-class district known for its teacher involvement, leadership and participation in the district's focus on collaboration and continuous improvement.

Setting up the teams

All three teams selected five teachers who they thought could represent teaching. We selected the researchers who we thought understood that the team was to work as a collaborative group – having a voice in decisions, learning how to collect data and sharing the responsibilities for doing so, and thinking hard together about what they found out when they looked together at the answers to their questions.

We also weighed in on the staff developers for BOCES and the union's team. We tried to select people who had worked with teachers in a development capacity, were good listeners, and could help turn the results of their questions into development activities for the rest of the school.

Learning about the research teams

Our hope was that teachers' knowledge, work and participation would be at the center. This would allow for getting at questions that do not oversimplify the teaching context. We hoped that spending time doing this work would also yield a sharing of what could be learned by teachers when they were in the majority on the team.

We were to find out that in two out of three of the teams, researchers took over and relegated teachers to be followers. (Of the three teams, Scarsdale represented the exception.) We learned that the researchers on the union and BOCES team seemed to feel that they knew more than the teachers about research so they should be responsible for making all the decisions about what to study, how to collect the data and what it all meant. This was the first time that raw power showed itself in this seemingly collaborative work. Teachers were clearly second-class citizens. Even in a team where teachers outnumbered the researchers, teachers were still thought of as objects of the researchers' work. We thought we had designed the perfect study where finally teachers' real lives could be represented.

What we learned about groups

From Scarsdale, empowered teachers were comfortable speaking out, taking responsibility, reading articles and books that talked about research, knew how to collaborate with others, and did not feel the difference in their roles in the group. They were also writers and ended up actually writing over 200 pages of what they had done on the team.

The other two groups were also great sources of what *we* learned. We learned that people who take different roles need to *learn* how to *collaborate*, how to represent their perspectives in a discussion, learn to take responsibilities in doing work that is new to them (how to phrase good questions; what kind of information needs to be collected and how much), how to sort the data when you get it, how to look for themes or examples that you can find in the data, and how to write about this work for an audience of their choice.

In summary:

1. Groups need to learn how to work together with those who have different positions and work.
2. Teachers need to learn how to represent their knowledge.
3. Teachers and others working together need to learn how to respect differences in knowledge.
4. All need to learn to trust and listen to one another.
5. All need to understand what others have to offer.

We came to understand a hugely important thing. Just forming a group – even when teachers outnumbered researchers and staff developers – was fine. But it was clearly not enough. People need to gain experience in being members of a collaborative group – and what that means. Different perspectives need to be expressed and the group needs to decide how they can be included in the work. People with different roles and different experience need to learn how to represent their ideas, negotiate with those who are in a team, and be respected for both their similarities and differences in thought and experience. Seven people (five teachers, one staff developer and one researcher) coming together do NOT make a collaborative group on their own. Collaboration and what it means needs to be learned by *all* members, particularly by those who have been in high-status positions. People need to be open to learning new ideas, without losing their perspectives. Groups such as these can and should have several people who can take leadership – not because of their status, but rather because facilitation of working together can be a shared idea.

We learned all this when we saw the Scarsdale team. It was teachers who worked WITH the researcher to create the research questions. The teachers on the team had written for publication and felt like equals to both the researcher and staff developer, and were involved in the entire process of doing the research and then writing about it. They had experience in collaborating earlier in their careers.

Just putting people together does not make a team, nor does it make possible teacher representation even though their numbers far exceeded the researcher and developer. These learnings happened in part because we were surprised that researchers took over and five teachers could not stop them. It never occurred to us that researchers felt the privilege of being the prime decision makers even though the team was to be "collaborative". We realized that collaboration is far more complicated than we thought. All on the team have to learn to participate, speak, learn new ideas, and figure out *together* how to do research as a collective team.

Expanding our knowledge

Several people began to write about ideas that taught us many things that deepened our understanding of groups - how they worked, what they worked on, the importance of experiential learning, and the whole idea of *group dynamics*. Kurt Lewin, a social psychologist fleeing Germany before World War II, eventually started a Center for Group Dynamics at MIT in the early 1940s. Although Lewin was a social psychologist, educators began to pick up the ideas he was working on as they had great relevance to education (Lewin, 1951). He coined the idea of *Field Theory*, which meant broadly that you needed to look at all the facts (in a group) as being mutually interdependent. These were important ideas as they called attention to not only different individuals' behaviors, but how they needed to be worked through together for the group to function effectively.

Lewin began to draw a variety of insights together from psychology and sociology, and although they were not from educational circles, they were picked up by educators as they had real relevance to the creation of groups and how they worked, how they were built, and what it really meant to be *collaborative*. Like the notions of "group pressures", "interdependence" and "task interdependence", these ideas were picked up by educators who began to work on and understand the complexities of community and collaboration. Lewin's oft-mentioned quote, "There is nothing more practical than a good theory", was also picked up by educators and encouraged the idea that theory AND practice could be related. He became famous for the idea that although people may come to a group with many different ways of thinking, if they share a common objective they are likely to act together to achieve it. *Group dynamics*, the way he explained it, was critical to understand. Groups can stimulate and motivate movement toward achieving common goals.

These ideas were picked up by educators as important to understand as much of the improvements at the time were group oriented. Change needs to be facilitated and guided as groups learn to work together. When this happens, people learn how to deal effectively with interpersonal relationships and make decisions together, regardless of their roles.

Lewin and Dewey were very connected in their views. They both felt that democracy must be learned in each generation. Lewin made the distinction between different kinds of groups, working with Lippitt (1949). They could be *democratic*, *autocratic*, or *laissez-faire*. In our study we assumed that the group members would be collaborative and treat each other as peers. But we learned that there was much learning to be done in order for that to happen. And much expertise was needed to make these groups democratic and cooperative.

The term "change agent" was created, which also added to our understanding. This person should understand the dynamics of groups, how to diagnose problems, plan for change, implement the plans and evaluate the results. Lewin wrote that to do this, the person must be emotionally involved, but also have a certain detachment so that the group could learn and develop. This was an important idea for educators – to be emotionally connected to what is going on, but be able to stand back and look objectively at the group you are leading.

The discovery and growth of action research

At the same time as Lewin, Stephen Corey (1949) began to write about *action research* for the first time. He had been at Teachers

College before my time and his ideas influenced both the curriculum and teaching. He organized a study which included looking at teachers' attitudes toward faculty meetings and found that they were *boring* and not meaningful for the teachers. Action research was another idea which was to involve teachers in creating a question that they wanted answered, collecting the data (How can I involve learners who are having difficulty keeping up?), and trying to solve the problem by gaining new information in their classroom.

Along with action research, there were many who began to take seriously the idea that we needed to learn how to collaborate, which some researchers realized was a complicated set of ideas. Again at Teachers College, Morton Deutsch (1949) focused his research on understanding how to build cooperation and competition as it appeared in groups.

Linking the task and the process of groups

Deutsch worked with Lewin and began his work describing the fact that the *task* (or *purpose*) and the *process* were critical to working with groups. He found that when these ideas meshed, they had important effects on the group. Members learned to communicate more, began to like each other more, and also tended to be more productive. Again, these ideas found their way into educational circles and had profound effects on group work.

Lewin created a Center for Group Dynamics at MIT and he attracted many researchers across the country. His ideas were so powerful because they resonated with both business and education as the ideas were intrinsic to their work. Groups and theory and research on groups was a critical part of the early 1950s. The idea that groups could study their own questions in search of answers involving greater complexity could help in the solution to social problems. *Field theory* became an important and powerful idea – as it described what makes groups work or falter. All these ideas eventually found their way into educational circles. And Teachers College had an important presence in both the invention of ideas and learning about groups.

References

Corey, S.M. (1949) Action research, fundamental research and educational practices. *Teachers College Record*, 50, 509–514

Deutsch, M. (1949) A theory of cooperation and competition. *Human Relations*, 2, 129–152.

Lewin, K. (1951) *Field Theory in Social Science: Selected Theoretical Papers* (D. Cartwright, ed.). New York: Harper and Row.

Lippitt, R. (1949) *Training in Community Relations*. New York: Harper and Row.

5

LEARNING FROM TEACHER LEADERS

Developing vignettes of the process

In the early 1980s after I had been a professor at Teachers College (TC) for over seven years I met Matthew Miles, a well-known quantitative researcher who had an office a few blocks from TC. He was interested in doing research in schools. He felt that he knew research and I knew schools and that we would be a good team. We could learn from one another and do some good work together. He was right. We clicked and easily taught each other what we knew and created some new innovative ideas as well.

At the time, school improvement was the rage. Everyone was doing something to engage teachers, create improvement strategies, and hopefully learn how better to teach students. There were three school improvement programs in New York City; each one was organized on different premises and possibilities for improvement. One program was run by the teachers' union in New York City – The American Federation of Teachers (AFT). They believed that the teachers should not only be a focus, but that the leadership in any improvements that the city was offering should be led by teachers. They had organized *Teacher Centers* in many schools run by union leadership and were situated in schools so that teachers could get ideas, support or conversation right in their own school. Another program had a Guru at the head who had his own particular ideas of what changes should be made and how they should go about it. The third one had a variety of prescriptions that needed to be followed for improvement to follow.

The study of three school improvement programs

We were hired to study these three improvement projects and find out how successful they were, and in what ways. The hope was that this would give the city some directions to proceed in. We created a general questionnaire and gave it to a large sample of teachers in all three programs. And we found out that all three were a mixed bag. Each one had a measure of success and clearly a measure of failure. So we set out to see if we could find out what the successes were and why they worked. We decided to interview a range of people in each program who had taken some form of leadership to see if we could unearth some data about their work to explain it to the city leadership and to the programs themselves. Not surprisingly, we found teachers in all three programs who had taken (or been given) leadership responsibilities in each professional development program.

A Teacher Center in the Bronx

We decided that each of us would take a different program and interview the teachers and then figure out what we could say. I began my part of the study by going to a Teacher Center in the Bronx run by one of the teacher union leaders. She was at the school before eight o'clock, and by the time she had gone to the fourth floor where the Teacher Center was located, she had already made three interventions with teachers to help them with their work. We finally arrived at the Center and I dutifully took out my ten interview questions which we had worked hard to create. We sat down in the Center and I began to ask her questions in the hope that I would finally get a sense of why teachers in leadership seemed to be successful at organizing professional development *with* teachers. I went through my entire list of ten interview questions. With each question, my interviewee would tell an incredible story which included history, context, professional and personal relationships, and more. And so it went. None of the interview answers revealed anything about the process of learning leadership or why their Teacher Center seemed to be successful, but the stories told of the complicated nature of the relationships in the school, in the district, and with teachers as well as the other complexities of the culture of the school and the problems of change.

Creating the vignette: Teachers as writers

I dutifully returned to work with Matt Miles in his office and told him that I had asked all my interview questions, but none of them were answered. However, I reported that there were many stories that were told about schools, teachers, working with teachers, the school culture, etc. What were we to do? How could we actually get at the leadership of the teachers who were successful in working at professional development in their school? What would give us the big ideas, but also the complicated surround that was obviously also very important to know? After much conversation, we realized that we would have to create a new method of getting data since the interview and questionnaire couldn't seem to pick up on why a particular teacher was successful with her colleagues, or what the process for engaging teachers in professional development looked like, or how the teachers developed leadership skills in the process of organizing work at the Teacher Center.

We developed the idea that teachers and teacher leaders could write their own story and maybe we could then get the full picture of professional development work and the process of learning to lead over time. We called our new tool the **vignette**. We reasoned that we could help the teachers frame what they were doing and with whom (in their writing) and if we got enough vignettes, we might be able to see some themes that would help us understand how leadership by teachers develops (Lieberman, 1987; Miles, Saxl, James, & Lieberman, 1986; Miles, Saxl, & Lieberman, 1988). How many vignettes would we need? How would we make them cogent, on the one hand, but also have the complexities of the growth process revealed? How would we report on the processes of *learning leadership*? Would we be able to convince the teachers who had developed leadership ability to **write**? There were no computers at this time!

We first realized that we could help the teachers frame the writing about their leadership by providing prompts that would help them stay on the task of writing about their leadership work and maybe confine their stories to the development of the process of how they learned to lead. It was a risk, but we were excited about trying it out. The vignette asked questions to frame the story. They included:

> What is the context of your school?
> What did you do? Or what did you hope would happen?
> Who was involved? (Who were you working with?)
> What happened as a result? (What was the reaction to your work?)
> What was the impact of your work?
> Why did it happen? (Document the reasons.)

As time went on and we used the vignette for other studies, we made the questions simpler and often used only four questions, depending on the situation. But it did indeed frame a "process" for growth which we were unable to get using the traditional research tools – an interview or questionnaire. We had no idea how many vignettes were needed, but in the beginning we found that fifteen of them gave us a good picture of the processes and tensions of developing leadership capacity.

What follows are two examples drawn from an earlier paper given at the American Educational Research Association many years ago describing the writing of two specialists (teachers who were leading Teacher Centers in New York City [Lieberman, 1987]). The teachers' union called their teacher leaders *teacher specialists*, trying to be sensitive to peers and the building of colleagueship, rather than creating another hierarchical role.

Lack of experience: Self-doubt – A vicious cycle

Parkview School was the "showcase" school in this particular district. It was a district that had recently changed from being primarily Italian and Jewish to now Black and Hispanic. There were approximately

1300 students in this elementary school. Because it had a good reputation in the district, many parents wanted to send their children there. As a result, the school was suffering serious overcrowding. Both new and experienced teachers were happy to come to this school as they felt that they would be in a very supportive environment. However, new teachers were usually quickly overwhelmed by the burden of high expectations placed on them, and self-doubt often plagued teachers new to the school. A group of new teachers had just arrived, as this school, like others in the area, was beginning to suffer a teacher shortage.

The teacher specialist, in this situation, wanted to help a new teacher who was having trouble by working with her in the classroom while linking her to a support group of other new teachers as well.

Who was involved

Louise, the focus of the specialist's work, was unmarried, in her mid-thirties and, up until then, had pursued a career in opera. She was softly spoken and very gentle and, although living in the area of the school, was clearly not "street wise".

She had been receiving "administrative" support, by way of cluster teachers (specialists in subject areas) and paraprofessionals coming into her classroom to model classroom management techniques on how to keep order. Louise often left the school in tears and eventually became ill, questioning whether she could ever "make it" as a teacher.

What she did

The specialist described the chain of events as she worked with this teacher. At first she had an "informal" lunch with her and other first grade teachers who had been in the school for a year. This led to her visiting the class. (Although Louise asked the specialist to tell her what was wrong, she was hoping for some positive feedback as well.) The specialist and Louise made a list together that included her strong points as well as where they thought improvement was needed. Over the course of the year, the specialist involved her in meetings, went to her class several times, modeled behavior that she thought would be helpful, encouraged her, in short – helped her survive in the classroom. She convinced Louise to participate in an institute during the summer where she would be exposed to behavioral and instructional management skills. The specialist and Louise met privately to write a list of rules, organize needed routines, arrange the furniture, etc. For the first few months of the semester, they continued to meet and Louise continued to need, and receive, reinforcement and practice in behavioral management.

The specialist sought to accomplish her goal of building up Louise's feelings of self-esteem (badly jeopardized by nagging doubts that she would never be able to teach) by working with her on classroom management as well as familiarizing her with the graded curriculum. She provided her with strategies to tie lessons together and to keep them moving at a pace that would help insure student participation.

Why it happened this way

Louise was able to grow professionally because she had come to teaching with a strong commitment and realized, early in her career, that she needed help. She was willing to listen, learn, adopt and adapt strategies to use in her classroom. The specialist, for her part, knew how to work with Louise to develop her sense of self, as well as to increase her knowledge and practices in learning the content and processes of working in a classroom. In addition, she created a support group for Louise and other new teachers – an innovation in that school – so that they would be able to continue to learn from and help each other.

Reading this vignette, I was reminded once again of the assault on one's sense of self that takes place during the first year of teaching – but we were able to see a long-term strategy that a teacher leader could use to help a new teacher survive and grow.

Introducing Learning Centers to an experienced teacher

In this vignette, the specialist described her school as a large elementary school with more than 1500 students who, as a whole, had low test scores. The faculty was characterized as having two factions who rarely communicated with each other. The majority of teachers used whole-class teaching methods with few provisions for looking at differences among students. The district had suggested Learning Centers, but few of the teachers had tried them. Most were resistant, claiming that they wouldn't work in their classrooms. In this case, the specialist was an expert in the use of Learning Centers.

Who was involved

The specialist's short-term goal was to re-introduce the idea of using Learning Centers in the first grade, while pursuing her long-term goal: to establish a network of teachers exchanging ideas, tasks and Learning Center methods, with the ultimate aim of improving teaching and learning in the school. Given the history of this school, these were very difficult goals.

The specialist decided to write down her goals so that she would stay on task herself and not be diverted. She also decided to communicate with the school administration so that they would know what she was doing and be available for needed support. She met with the District Coordinator to influence district-wide staff development plans so that they would reflect a greater sensitivity to teacher needs. Lastly, the specialist was able to get the district to change its policy from a *suggested use* of Learning Centers to an **attempt** to use them. She thought this change might encourage more teachers interested in developing Learning Centers to try them, while forestalling a mandate which could be detrimental to the whole effort.

Initially, the specialist singled out Mrs. B as a focus for her efforts. She was well respected in the school yet, at the same time, the most negative about Learning Centers. It was a calculated risk, but the specialist figured that if she could convince her, the word would spread. Mrs. B. was regarded as a leader, very frank and outspoken. She used the whole-class method and had already voiced her view that it would not work with her students.

What the specialist did

The specialist used her understanding and knowledge of adult development to plan her approach. She knew that Mrs. B would have to be in charge if she was going to try anything new. Fortunately, Mrs. B. regarded the specialist as both a colleague and friend. First, the specialist helped clear some erroneous notion held by Mrs. B. that Learning Centers were only for gifted and well-behaved students. Then Mrs. B. was selected to be involved in a team teaching situation. She was able to go to a series of workshops on "How to Effectively Team Teach". She was to have fifteen students and two teachers in the class. And she was clearly in a leadership position. After three team meetings, Mrs. B. asked the specialist to explain to her and the other first grade teachers about Learning Centers.

Mrs. B. finally asked her team mate if she would be interested in giving Learning Centers a try. The specialist worked with the two of them on a steady basis for almost a month, teaching them how to select a topic, what materials to use, how to make the materials, purchase supplies, etc.

What happened as a result

Mrs. B. became actively involved in the use of Centers in her classroom. She invited the principal into her room and he publicly complimented her. Follow-up meetings were held during common prep times arranged by the administration.

The impact

The specialist's success was dramatically illustrated when Mrs. B. both thanked her and blamed her in the same breath – blame for having allowed her to deprive her students of learning opportunities for so long, and thanks for bringing back to her, after fourteen years, the excitement of teaching. Mrs. B's leadership, both direct and by example, led the other teachers to try Learning Centers – with both the specialist and Mrs. B providing the technical and personal support necessary for implementing this district-wide initiative.

The power of using vignettes

We were made aware of dramatic descriptions dealing with tough problems in difficult environments as well as the eventual willingness to take initiatives with support from specialists who encouraged feelings of enhanced professionalism, and saw it in teachers' practice. Specialists were learning along the way how to involve teachers and, at the same time, deal with cultural barriers that stood in the way of the complicated process of change.

We were convinced that the vignette was a promising tool for collecting data. Its power and value lies in the subtleties and nuances of character and the organizational detail that only an insider, living the events as they unfold over time, can express. We learned that the vignette written by an insider included the complexities of teaching and learning.

Expanding our knowledge

In the 1980s and beyond, a new surge of research and writing began to examine far more closely why improvements in schools were fraught with such difficulty (Lieberman, 1987). Some researchers began to look more skeptically at professional development and the kind of organizational conditions that were necessary, including the inevitable tensions of trying to change teaching within different kinds of school climates.

Little (1986) described most convincingly that ideas such as collaboration, cooperation, partnerships, etc. were far more complicated than anyone had thought. Collegiality demanded a variety of organizational conditions that we were only beginning to realize were challenging, both to do, to lead and to sustain. She began to describe the differences that teachers felt when they were to be "trained" rather than asked to *participate*. She also called attention to the fact that many professional development ideas paid little attention to the amount of time needed for teachers to practice, much less be involved in "collective participation", which was not part of the regular practice of most schools and needed to be learned.

At the same time, McLaughlin has consistently reminded us that "Policy can't mandate what matters most: what matters most is *local capacity and will*" (1987, p.172). This involves local expertise, organizational routines and resources available to support teacher and student learning. And these things change over time. Teachers' *will* and motivation is contingent on the kind of support they get, how they are engaged, and whether there is sufficient time and help to learn new skills, abilities and pedagogies. Their involvement is dependent on the larger social and political context within which they live and work. Our examples show more explicitly what these mean in practice.

For others, the idea of starting with teachers became a powerful and important theme:

> *We need to think about the complex interplay among different aspects of an organization before, during, and after implementation of new policies and programs. School improvement ought to emphasize building from within. Those of us who claim to be wizards ought to make sure that our primary role is to help people see the power that they themselves have to make things better.*
>
> *(Deal, 1986, p. 127)*

References

Deal, T.E. (1986) Educational change: Revival tent, tinkertoys, jungle or carnival. In Lieberman, A. (Ed.), *Rethinking School Improvement: Research, Craft and Concept*. New York: Teachers College Press, pp. 115–128.

Lieberman, A. (Ed.) (1986) *Rethinking School Improvement: Research, Craft and Concept*. New York: Teachers College Press.

Lieberman, A. (1987) *Documenting Professional Practice: The Vignette as a Qualitative Tool*. Paper given at the American Educational Research Association. April, 14 pages.

Little, J.W. (1986) Seductive images and organizational realities in professional development. In Lieberman, A. (Ed.), *Rethinking School Improvement: Research, Craft and Concept*. New York: Teachers College Press, pp. 26–44.

McLaughlin, M.W. (1987) Learning from experience: Lessons from policy implementation. *Educational Evaluation and Policy Analysis*, 9(2), 171–178.

Miles, M., Saxl, E.R., James, J.A., & Lieberman, A. (1986) *New York City Teacher Centers Consortium Evaluation Report, 1985–86*. New York: Center for Policy Research.

Miles, M., Saxl, E.R., & Lieberman, A. (1988) Key skills of educational "change agents": An empirical view. *Curriculum Inquiry*, 18(2), 157–193.

6

TEACHERS AS SCHOLARS

Getting at the complexity of teaching

It's not a castle surrounded by a moat
It has no walls, it has no towers
Made of professional knowledge work and hope
And a community of scholars it empowers
  Make it public
  Critique it
  Build upon it
  Pass it on

For ten years, I worked at the Carnegie Foundation for the Advancement of Teaching where Tom Hatch and I were in charge of working
with k-12 teachers and teacher educators. We were initially trying to
understand how teachers could become scholars. What would that
mean? What would it look like? How could we demonstrate it? What
forms would it take? As we were struggling to figure it out, I was
constantly telling my husband (a songwriter) what we were doing at
Carnegie and how we were trying to figure out what the Scholarship
of Teaching and Learning was. He wrote us a song (above), which we
all learned (our staff and the cohorts of teachers and teacher educators
with whom we worked) (Lieberman, 2000). It captures the meaning

of the Scholarship of Teaching and Learning (SOTL) that became the focus of our work.

The Carnegie Foundation was dealing with the SOTL for higher education and we were dealing with scholarship as something that k–12 teachers could aspire to as well. The first thing we did was to bring a cohort of excellent teachers and teacher educators to Carnegie to struggle with us to understand, discuss and hopefully demonstrate what scholarship looked like when we collaborated with teachers. From the beginning, this was an exceptional group. Often you couldn't tell who was a teacher, a teacher educator, or a Carnegie person. We built the most powerful collaborative team where each group had important ideas to add to our struggle to understand "scholarship", particularly in k–12.

The meaning of the Scholarship of Teaching and Learning

Lee Shulman, president of Carnegie, conceptualized what he thought the SOTL might entail. For him, it was a combination of *professionalism, pragmatism and policy* (Shulman, 2000).

Professionalism meant that knowledge should be shared and passed on and exchanged with others publically. It also meant that there was constant improvement in the interests of student learning. And lastly, it meant that policies could respond to the demands of the market even as they enabled professional practice.

Shulman contributed significantly to the discussion that teaching needed to become *community property*, an idea that he had written about earlier (Shulman, 1993, 2011). When he wrote about this in 1993, he posited three strategies that scholars in higher education needed to develop. First and foremost, we needed to "reconnect teaching to the disciplines" as a way of making teaching valued; second, "we must capture the artifacts to demonstrate its richness and complexity", and lastly, "if we deem it [teaching] valuable, it must be open to judgement by others". These strategies, if developed, would help make teaching not only community property, but far more open to "scholarship" as recognized in higher education.

Starting with teaching practice: Engaging in "scholarship"

To begin to think about what the scholarship of teaching in k–12 meant, we invited a group of teachers and teacher educators with excellent reputations to work together with us at Carnegie to figure out what *scholarship* looked like, how it could be described, and what we could learn together about k–12 teaching that could lend itself to a deeper understanding of SOTL. In some ways, we were trying to describe what Lampert (2001) painstakingly described in her brilliant book, *Teaching Problems and the Problems of Teaching*.

> *One reason teaching is a complex practice is that many of the problems a teacher must address to get students to learn occur simultaneously . . . Because of this simultaneity, several different problems must be addressed by a single action. Problems exist across social, temporal, and intellectual domains, and often actions that need to be taken to solve problems are different in different domains.*
>
> *(Lampert, 2001, p. 2)*

For openers, we knew that we had to build a partnership with a group of teachers who would be willing to go public with their work, describe how it looked in their classrooms, what they hoped the students would learn, and what the "artifacts" that Shulman talked about looked like as we worked together.

We knew we had to build a collaborative culture at Carnegie and, as a team, figure out what SOTL was for k–12. In our quest to work with teachers, we knew we had to find a way to describe all the complexities of what it means to teach and what it looks like. How could we do this? What would allow us to both *show* the complexity and *tell* what we could do that would further explain what might be considered the scholarship of teaching?

We were incredibly fortunate in having Desirée Pointer Mace as a member of our team, who was a second-generation "techie" and extraordinarily talented with the computer, what it could do and how one could develop an online set of teacher practices. She knew things about the computer that none of us had ever experienced or even understood at the time. And she began to think about what we might do online that would begin to address our quest for getting at the complexities of teaching in a different way (Pointer Mace, 2009). One of the things she taught us was that online it might be possible to get at showing teaching and even writing something that viewers could read that enhanced what one was seeing online. You could actually show a teacher and their students, and you could write where the idea came from, and something about the teacher's background and their ideas and strategies about teaching. This was a radical idea when we began to embrace this concept (see insideteaching.org)! We all began to realize that perhaps putting teaching online could help us solve the eternal question of getting at the complexities of teaching, but we were naïve about what it might look like, and how you could explain the complexities that we had all experienced and written about.

Pointer Mace began to think about what we should put online so that we could *tell* and *show* what the complexities of teaching look like. She conceptualized for all of us what we should do to create websites with a variety of teachers from k-12. Here is what she wrote:

The important pieces to include in a k-12 multi-media case for use in preservice education and professional development

Ideally, the websites will have multiple entry points into each teachers' teaching practice, with relevance within and across grade levels and subject matter areas.

Introduction

- Introductory paragraph – the teacher and the work, what can be found on the site.
- A way to contact the teacher (email, forum, etc.).

Documentation of teaching practice

- Documentation from beginning, middle and end of the year.
- Shorter video clips with annotation juxtaposed with longer video clips that can be "mined" by others.

Reflection on teaching practice

- Reflective video or narratives about the evidence collected on the page (classes videotaped, etc.).
- Reflective video or narrative pieces about the practitioner's journey and sense of professional presence.
- Reflective video of teacher talking about the development of the strategies seen in the documentation.
- Reflection on inquiry/questions framing and informing the teacher's practice.
- Observations about outcomes (student learning, assessment, achievement).

Intellectual context and materials

- Links to resources/literature/other examples of practice that inform the teacher's thinking.
- Articles, narratives written by the teacher about the specific strategies involved in the teaching excerpts.

Pedagogical context and materials

- Teacher's philosophy and goals and how those connect to practice.
- Some sense of the evolution of practice.
- Context: description of the school, classroom, community.
- How these videotaped vignettes fit into the larger course/year – what came before and after.
- Examples of materials used in class (like the anticipation guide).
- Strategies made visible: what was used? How was it used? How was it developed?
- How do strategies and practices fit into a larger context of practice?
- Particular strategies or pedagogical choices/documents or tools that inform your year-long practice (such as Yvonne's stock questions).
- Any relevant school/district documents that inform the practice.

Students

- Context of the students – who are they?
- Images/examples of student work.
- Multiple drafts of student work that show struggles and growth.
- Student work that shows the variability of student performance.

Little did we know then that technology could help us solve the problem of the complexities of teaching. We then began to struggle with different questions such as: What do you select for viewing? How do you make the complexities of teaching simple enough without minimizing its complicated nature? How much needs to be made public? And how much do you need to show?

How much to tell? Pointer Mace (2009) was to continue to connect technology to teaching as she built upon the knowledge of a variety of teachers online.

Using Pointer Mace's description of what should be in a multimedia case, we describe two multimedia sites – one by a secondary teacher, Yvonne Hutchinson, and the other by an elementary teacher, Sarah Capitelli – both teachers in our Carnegie group. Both sites are available at insideteaching.org.

The two teachers here are a small representation of what the public can find on insideteaching.org. We learned together how to *tell* things like a teacher's background, philosophy and purposes in their teaching. And we learned what we needed to *show* so that viewers could see both the background material that helped the teacher think about her teaching and the actual teaching lesson that would show teaching without leaving out any of the important things that a teacher tucks in, rather than talks about.

Yvonne Hutchinson was a secondary English teacher while Sarah Capitelli taught first/second graders in an elementary school.

Yvonne tells us that she is going to put a "class anatomy" online that describes one of her classes. She gives us six video clips which describe what happens in the classroom. We immediately read that she is building on the oral traditions of her African-American and Latino students. We learn what is on the site from her written description. We hear her description of what she wants from the

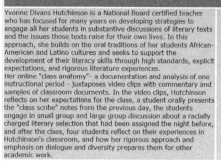

A Friend of Their Minds: Capitalizing on the Oral Tradition of My African American Students
CLASS ANATOMY

YVONNE DIVANS HUTCHINSON
KING-DREW MEDICAL MAGNET SCHOOL
LOS ANGELES, CA

Yvonne Divans Hutchinson is a National Board certified teacher who has focused for many years on developing strategies to engage all her students in substantive discussions of literary texts and the issues those texts raise for their own lives. In this approach, she builds on the oral traditions of her students African-American and Latino cultures and seeks to support the development of their literacy skills through high standards, explicit expectations, and rigorous literature experiences.

Her online "class anatomy"- a documentation and analysis of one instructional period - juxtaposes video clips with commentary and samples of classroom documents. In the video clips, Hutchinson reflects on her expectations for the class, a student orally presents the "class scribe" notes from the previous day, the students engage in small group and large group discussion about a racially charged literary selection that had been assigned the night before, and after the class, four students reflect on their experiences in Hutchinson's classroom, and how her rigorous approach and emphasis on dialogue and diversity prepares them for other academic work.

Context and Reflections

1. Thinking with Text
2. Project Snapshot
3. Teaching Context: School and Students
4. Video: What audiences of this work should know about Yvonne's teaching, and her journey to develop this approach.
5. Narrative: Where I Began/ Where I Began

Materials and Strategies

1. Strategies for Promoting Literate Discourse
2. Question-Answer Relationships • Student Response Sample
3. Anticipation Guide
4. Reading Response Prompt
5. Class Scribe Prompt • Class Scribe Writing Sample
6. Informal Reading Assessment

Video:
Entire class session (2 hours)
Entire reflective interview (1 hour)

How they got here:
The beginning of the school year
<<<<

Class Anatomy Timeline

Class Session: June 2002

Where they went next:
The following school year
>>>>

1. Setting Goals for the Class Session

YDH tells what she expects to see as evidence of oral discourse as students discuss a memoir by Willie Ruff, "A Call to Assembly." . (4:00)

2. Describing the Previous Day's Work

DJ, class scribe for the previous day, delivers his lively and humorous narrative of the class activities for that day. At the end of the report, his peers evaluate both the report and his delivery. Daily class scribe reports and related instructional materials or handouts are kept in a Class Notebook in the classroom. (3:03)

3. Engaging in Small Group Discussion

Responding to teacher's directions to honor diversity in their choices of discussion partners, students meet in duos or trios to share their responses to the Anticipation Guide for "A Call to Assembly." (6:03)

4. Connecting to Larger Societal Issues

Andrea speaks passionately about leaders from African American and Hispanic communities and the difficulties of effecting change. She ends her talk with an indictment of Black and Hispanic gangs and the diviseness among (and between) the two racial groups. (3:41)

5. Making Explicit Reference to the Text

Gladis begins the discussion of a pivotal moment in the text, questioning the use of the perjorative "N" word. Tiffany shows discernment in her analysis of the ten year old Ruff's motive in quitting his job. Other students voice their ideas, and the conversation culminates with Ashlan sharing her knowledge of sign language. (3:41)

6. Reflecting on the Impact of Diversity, Rigor, and Discourse

Dejean, Andrea, Tiffany reveal how the requirement to honor diversity in their classroom interactions not only broadened their perspective, but resulted in new friendships. (1:44)

FIGURE 6.1 Yvonne Hutchinson: Class anatomy of a high school Teacher

students in this particular lesson. (You can read the anticipation guide, which helps students get into the story and the context.) In clip 2 we hear about yesterday's class so we see the connection between yesterday and today. In clip 3 she organizes the class by having them choose different partners than their usual or comfortable ones to help form discussion groups.

They are reading a portion of a memoir by Willie Ruff, *A Call to Assembly*. By clip 4 the students have read the text and speak about the difficulties of racial harmony. In clip 5 the discussion continues about the use of the "N" word. In clip 6 the students reflect on their own behavior. We see the pedagogical context and Hutchinson's use of materials. The reader is "told" about the materials and strategies as well as Hutchinson's background and how she has developed this particular lesson. What we see is a great example of how one can "show" the complexities of teaching and "tell" some of the background, and reveal some of the materials (such as the anticipation guide). In real terms, what we see on video is actually how Hutchinson prepares the students through the use of the guide, has them choose to sit in a more diverse group (thereby living some of the issues that they are reading about), and chooses a literary piece where they see in real life the kind of controversy and problems of racism and racial diversity.

After they have read the piece, she asks them to discuss their views. The students respond by talking about their own experience on the one hand, and referring to the text on the other. In the process, Hutchinson reveals how to connect a piece of literature to the experiences of her students. She also shows us how she prepares the students for the lesson (through the anticipation guide about their own experiences and how they connect to the literary piece that they read).

Sarah Capitelli is an elementary school teacher (first/second grade). She is trying to teach her English language learners how to speak better English. She organizes a variety of situations where students learn by being led by those who speak well, who are helping those who are still learning. What we learn from her site is the variety of opportunities Capitelli organizes, the strategies she creates and how, when she uses those who speak better as leaders for others, what each student learns in the process. For Capitelli, part of what she "shows" is how video can be used to enhance one's English, and how

Learning from our conversations in English: Using video in the bilingual classroom as a tool for reflection on English language learning and teaching

Sarah Capitelli, **Melrose Elementary School, Oakland CA**
with Desiree Pointer, Knowledge Media Lab, The Carnegie Foundation

How we learned from our conversations in English:

1. Overview
2. What structures support English language development in my classroom?
3. How do conversations between students support English language learning?
4. What structures do good English language learners use?
5. How can video be used to improve students to reflect on their own English language learning?
6. Next steps

Context
- About me and my class, and my inquiry

Class Materials
- List of the kind of student written video report
- I show myself a later time
- Sample Interview scripts

Resources
- Video presentation about the major work that led me to this project
- First Year Narratives [PDF]
- First Year Analysis [PDF]
- Poster presented at our work at AERA

Overview

I am a 1st/2nd Spanish bilingual teacher in Oakland, California. This snapshot tells part of the story of my inquiry journey in my classroom. The work that is represented here comes in the middle of a longer story that began when I started teaching five years ago and continues as I am learning to become a better teacher and teacher researcher. Since beginning my teaching career I have been concerned with how to best meet the needs of my English language learners (ELL) during English language development (ELD) class. In particular, I am concerned with how to help them create a strong foundation for their learning of English. In my research I have discovered that our school's program has not worked for the most needy students. For this reason I have continued to study my own ELD practice. This snapshot is an example of my inquiry project last year in my ELD class. My research questions were 1) what structures support communication between students during ELD? and 2) how do conversations impact their English language learning?

Based on my prior research I structured a new program last year in which I had a heterogeneous ELD class and organized multiple opportunities for students to talk with one another in English. The idea guiding this practice was that by talking with one another, students could help one another learn to speak English. The more experienced English speakers could assist those less conversant and in doing so learn more English themselves. Throughout the process I collected various kinds of data including student work, narratives of practice and student achievement data. I also experimented using video data to better understand what was really going on in my students' conversations. I have included conversations between students, conversations with colleagues, student work, classroom conversations and my own reflections on these pieces of text.

As a teacher researcher who is new to using video in her classroom, I have come to see video as an inquiry tool for both the students and myself that provides the class with new windows through which to reflect upon English language learning and teaching. My hope is that this snapshot will provide others with a window into both my ongoing processes of teacher inquiry and learning, as well as their own inquiry and learning.

(Note: This site requires the Quicktime and Flash plugins.)

(Mouse over the photos to see the evolution of my inquiry, click to see videos, context narratives, and reflections.)

FIGURE 6.2 Sarah Capitelli: Learning from a first/second grade bilingual teacher

it can be used for the students as a form of inquiry into getting better at expressing themselves. She learned to use video for the students, but also for herself, as she learned to see (and reflect on) how the students struggled with the language, how the better speakers who were close to their friends could be helpful as leaders, and what seemed to her to need more work.

She "tells" us what structures she learns to use in the process as well as what those who speak well use. Then by using video she enhances both the students' learning, and her own as well.

We also learn about her school, her particular class and how her inquiry is aided by learning how to use video as an important tool in teaching English language learners. We also learn that Sarah organized her learning and wrote a paper, which she presented at AERA.

Expanding our knowledge

Sancho (2010) makes the powerful point that digital technologies are having a powerful influence on new generations of children and are clearly changing how knowledge is conceived, used and valued. Technology has changed the culture of young people, their "views on life, values, ways of learning and modes of accessing knowledge" (p.435). But interestingly, schools and school systems have been very slow to realize that changes in the society have changed students' expectations and have even become disconnected from the lives of the students they teach. Students are heavily involved with mobile phones, tablets, computers and more, but school structures have not been able to keep up with these changes in attitudes, relationships as well as the knowledge that students pick up as they engage in technology.

However, this seems to have changed in the last decade outside of school. Both the values as well as how knowledge is displayed and organized has changed in developed countries. Now recreation, movies, sports, news in homes, as well as the use of technology in hospitals, agriculture and a variety of companies, is ubiquitous. As Sancho (2010) puts it, "new information and communication technologies alter our interests, the nature of how we think as well as the nature of our communities" (p.435).

Although these changes result in global transformation, schools remain hardly changed at all. Sancho believes that although the world has rapidly changed technologically, students do not feel engaged in schooling because their lives are so different to what they are engaged in at school. The challenges are many: maintaining social cohesion, engaging students in personal and social projects, updating educators' knowledge, as well as bridging the past with future knowledge (p.441).

Michael Apple (2010) focuses on the social uses of the internet and calls our attention to how movements grow and support themselves – in this case, how technological resources can serve a multitude of social agendas. He writes about the conservative Christian evangelicals and makes a case for how the connections between curriculum and the new politics of knowledge are used. The new technologies create a social and ideological context for different groups to solidify their influence. He expands our understanding of how technology can be used to influence social and political ideas – not just the normal subjects we associate with public schooling.

68 Teachers as scholars

References

Apple, M. (2010) *The Emerging Politics of Curriculum Reform: Technology Knowledge, and Power in Homeschooling.* In Hargreaves, A., Lieberman, A., Fullan, M., & Hopkins, D. (Eds.), *Second Handbook of Educational Change.* Dordrecht: Kluwer Academic Publishers, pp. 913–931.

Hatch, T., Ahmed, D., Lieberman, A., Faigenbaum, D., Eiler White, M., & Pointer Mace, D.H. (Eds.) (2005) *Going Public with our Teaching: An Anthology of Practice.* New York: Teachers College Press

Lampert, M. (2001) *Teaching Problems and the Problems of Teaching.* New Haven, CT: Yale University Press.

Lieberman, E. (2000) The CASTL song.

Pointer Mace, D. (2009) *Teacher Practice Online: Sharing Wisdom, Opening Doors.* New York: Teachers College Press.

Sancho, J.M. (2010) Digital technologies and educational change. In Hargreaves, A., Lieberman, A., Fullan, M., & Hopkins, D. (Eds.), *The Second Handbook of Educational Change.* New York: Springer, pp. 433–444.

Shulman, L. (1993) Teaching as community property. *Change,* 25(6), 6–7.

Shulman, L. (2000) From Minsk to Pinsk: Why a Scholarship of Teaching and Learning? *Journal of Scholarship of Teaching and Learning,* 1(1), 48–53.

Shulman, L. (2011) Feature essays: The Scholarship of Teaching and Learning: A personal account and reflection. *International Journal for the Scholarship of Teaching and Learning,* 5(1), Article 30.

7

CREATING THE CONDITIONS FOR LEARNING AND LEADERSHIP

The National Writing Project

In the 1990s, many people had mentioned that we should really study the National Writing Project (NWP). I had heard of it but knew nothing about it, its purposes, practices or possibilities. I only knew that it seemed to be spreading all over the United States. Many teachers who I spoke with who had gone to the Summer Institute of the National Writing Project would answer with the same refrain. When you asked them what they thought of the summer institute, they would say it is like "magic". I knew that it had to do with improving writing, but I had no idea what the NWP did and why teachers were so enthusiastic about their connections to it. What could the "magic" be? Could we find it and describe it in concrete terms that we would all understand?

I was at Teachers College as a professor and asked Diane Wood if she was interested in working with me if I could get the NWP to let us study what they were doing, and hopefully why teachers were so excited about their participation in the NWP. I knew they were developing different sites all over the United States, and I knew that teachers raved about their participation. But I had no idea about what they did when teachers actually went to the summer institute, anywhere from two to five weeks during the summer. I was intrigued by the teachers' responses as they were excited and extremely enthusiastic about their participation. What was going on during those weeks? Could we actually nail what made the teachers think it was "magic"? I was friendly with Richard Sterling, who was the head of the NWP at the time, and told him that I would like to do research on the NWP to find out what the summer institute was all about and why teachers consistently raved about participating in it. Everyone I spoke with said to study the summer institute. It all happens there.

Making friends with the NWP

I spoke with a few others who were in NWP leadership and they suggested looking at two different sites – one that had been going for a long time, and one that was fairly new. They thought that would give a sense of what the basic elements were, how routines were developed, and possibly how it had become influential all over the United States. So I set about finding out what was possible and how we could negotiate a study where we could document the summer institute and why teachers spoke of it as having a "magical quality". Since I had never studied "magic" before, it seemed like a fascinating study, yet one that might be tough to penetrate. But we thought that the questions we developed would be interesting to the NWP as well as to those interested more broadly in the professional development of teachers. The NWP leadership was united behind the idea that "it all happens in the summer institute".

Many people knew of the NWP but not much detail about it. But all seemed to know that it seemed to be very successful. We did not meet anyone who could tell us what goes on in the summer institute, so that seemed like a natural first question. It seemed like if you were interested in teacher learning and leadership (which I was), this should be studied so I wrote a proposal and luckily got the study funded. Now all Diane and I had to do was figure out with the NWP just exactly *what* we were going to study and *how* we were going to find out the mystical quality of the summer institute.

Studying two sites: Old and new

The NWP leadership suggested that we study the site in Los Angeles (housed at UCLA), which had been going for twenty years, where routines and activities were well organized, and also Oklahoma State in Stillwater (OSU), where there was a relatively new "site" which was only seven years old. They all felt that this would make an interesting comparison and that we would see just exactly why the teachers were so enthusiastic, how it was organized and why teachers immediately responded to what went on there. Hopefully we would learn what goes on at the summer institute, what appear to be the routines that involve the teachers who come there and what it is about the time spent together that made the teachers feel that "this is the best professional development ever".

The LA site was clearly in an urban area, and the Oklahoma site was a mixture of rural and suburban so we could also see how the contexts differed and how that might affect the teachers. We were interested in activities that involved the teachers, and how they became engaged both individually and collectively. What, if anything, seemed to bind them together in some kind of community? We quickly learned that the site was in a college or university and run by a person at the university, often with a teacher (or a teacher advisory group) comprising the leadership team.

I took the UCLA and the LA "site" (where there was an office for the NWP) as I was most familiar with it, having gone there as an undergraduate and doctoral student, and Diane took Oklahoma State. We both went to our respective summer institutes for the entire time so we could document what went on for the five weeks, figuring that together we could work out the "magic". The co-director (Elyse Eidman-Aadahl) told us that the "work" of the NWP was really the "enactment of a culture". Needless to say, we were anxious to figure out what she meant and hoped that observing the whole institute would reveal the answers.

Creating a model: Observing the summer institute

During the year, writing project leaders seek out teachers who teach writing as part of their English curriculum in elementary and secondary schools. Although Jim Gray, the founder of the NWP, was a secondary English teacher, teachers of all k-12 students come to the summer institute. We found that there are three core activities that govern the model of the NWP.

- Creating forums for successful teachers to teach one another.
- Engaging teachers in reading and discussing relevant educational literature and research.
- Providing opportunities for teachers to write and share their writing in response groups.

(Gray, 2000)

The evolution of the NWP

Jim Gray, a high school English teacher, wrote about how he kept trying to convince his principal that they didn't need outsiders to tell them how to improve. Why not organize the insiders and let them teach each other? Gray, teaching at San Leandro High School in California, was convinced that "insiders", teachers, had a tremendous amount of success with their students. Why couldn't they teach each other what had worked in their classrooms? Why couldn't they share all those successful strategies and techniques that teachers had worked on over their whole careers with their fellow teachers? How could opportunities for teachers to teach teachers be organized? In this way, the teachers could learn from one another – they could be teachers, learners and leaders all at the same time. There were articles written in the 1970s about why students couldn't write, so Gray took advantage of the interest and got support from the University of California at Berkeley (where he had supervised students for thirteen years), to start what he called *The Bay Area Summer Institute for the Teaching of Writing*.

Gray organized twenty-nine teachers to come together on the Berkeley Campus. With the university's partnership they proceeded to work with a new central idea: *teacher knowledge was to be the starting point for learning*. There would be a new set of principles and organizational ideas:

- A "site" is a group of local teachers in partnership with a university or college.
- Teachers would teach one another their "best practices".

- Teachers would write and present their own work.
- Teachers would read, discuss, and analyze research, reforms and other literature.

(Lieberman and Wood, 2003)

That first institute at Berkeley was so successful that Gray immediately began to respond to other places which could hold an institute based on what he had done, raising money along the way. Interestingly, the principles were easy to organize, easy to prepare for, and easy to implement. It was clear that the big idea was that teachers were writing *their* stories, working on *their writing*, and teaching *their best lessons* to their peers. What were they learning about bettering their writing? How were they using this *inside knowledge* in their classrooms? Could the NWP actually be playing out a program that created professional learning and leadership where "teaching practice" was the starting point for learning? We were about to find out answers to these questions.

Inside the summer institute

I came equipped with lots of paper and a pen to write down everything I was seeing in Moore Hall (at UCLA). About twenty teachers strolled in and I quickly got the idea that they shared things with each other as they took turns bringing things for teachers to eat during the day. During the five weeks, we came to understand how teachers became committed to their own improvement. We first listed all the things we saw (and talked together every night comparing notes). And in a few months of discussion, we finally realized that we were seeing a set of practices, which taken together totally involved teachers in sharing their own work and then opening up to others – their colleagues and to other authors doing research. As they wrote, got feedback, taught their favorite lessons, listened to others, read and critiqued research, they were learning all the time. We were to struggle to understand how these conditions that existed during the summer institute radically switched the way we thought about teacher learning. In the NWP, it was not about "telling" people how to change their practice, but rather about engaging each other in how to "show" what they were writing and teaching, giving feedback to make it better, exposing people to other teachers' practices, learning together by reading research and other articles, and learning how to critique constructively and learn from the outside too – all the time writing and going public with their own practices and their knowledge that they had accrued over time.

The social practices of the NWP

As we observed both sites, we realized that there was so much going on that continued to add to teachers' sense of themselves, their writing, their learning and their teaching. We finally described all the things we saw happening during the summer institute as a set of social practices. These included:

- **Approaching each colleague as a potentially valuable contributor.**
- **Honoring teacher knowledge.**
- **Creating public forums for teacher sharing, dialogue and critique.**
- **Turning ownership of learning over to the learners.**
- **Situating human learning in practice and relationships.**
- **Providing multiple entry points into the learning community.**
- **Guiding reflection on teaching, through reflection on learning.**
- **Sharing leadership.**
- **Promoting an inquiry stance.**
- **Encouraging a reconceptualization of professional identity and linking it to professional community.**

(Lieberman and Wood, 2003, p.22)

We came to realize that these practices were interactive and mutually dependent, and when experienced together created an important learning community for the teachers – perhaps for the first time in their teaching lives. We also finally understood why the NWP had not had a researcher study them for years. It is important to see that the strategy for coming together is to use the work and life of a teacher (rather than a researcher) to display teaching practice by having the participants both teach and learn from one another, and to write, get critiqued, and write some more to understand what it takes to write well. In some ways, this was the opposite of how researchers would work. They would ask questions from the outside/in, rather than what Gray had in mind, to have the questions emanate from the inside/out. Teachers teaching teachers was a radical idea, even though it happens all the time. In the summer institute this was a central idea.

All of these practices helped elevate not only the NWP, but the idea that practitioner knowledge was a badly needed perspective in issues of school reform and development. Teachers learned in the summer institute that they could apply many of the social practices in their own classrooms. Many learned that they could build a community in their room and have students experience learning by working on their own writing with critique and help from their fellow students (as they had done during the summer institute). Many teachers began to see themselves and their work differently as they experienced putting their practice at the center, recognizing that what they knew and produced as writers was the starting point for their own involvement, understanding and eventual improvement (St. John, Dickey, Hirabayashi and Stokes, 2001). And what we learned was that you could create the conditions for continuous learning by starting with what teachers had learned and practiced in their own classrooms. They could then expand that learning by looking at research and other people's knowledge.

Expanding our knowledge

While we were learning about the NWP, a number of researchers were learning about a variety of ways for teachers to be involved in learning by using their own practices. Wenger (1998), coining the term "communities of practice", wrote a very influential book (by the same name) making popular the idea that learning is actually "social participation" and that people who participate in communities literally construct their identities, and shape "not only what we do" but "who we are" (p.4).

Wenger was not writing about education or schools, but his ideas became an important way of describing not only the NWP but why and how communities were so critical to learning. He connected conceptually much of what we were seeing in the NWP. In education, his idea of using meaning, practice, community and identity was another way of explaining why and how the summer institute was such an important phenomenon for teachers. Much of teaching life is in isolation and learning by doing. But Wenger was to give meaning to the importance of community because for him learning had everything to do with learning as doing, learning by experience, as well as learning as belonging. Community, rather than isolation, was a key to learning. It was his work that provided the deeper understanding of what was happening in the summer institute. And for teachers, this turned out to be a rare opportunity to learn from colleagues as they build (over time) a community based on their everyday practices. We began to understand why the teachers were all saying that the NWP was like magic!

Cochran-Smith and Lytle (1993) importantly documented the growth of teacher research in education. They too, like the NWP, were concerned with knowledge about teaching that was inside/out, that is, knowledge that teachers constructed when they studied their own practice. In a way, they built the idea that teachers could be the researchers of their own work, rather than being researched from the outside. They described teacher research as inquiry into practice, turning teachers to studying their own work and thereby opening them up to developing and improving their practice from the *inside.*

Earlier, Karl Weick (1979) expressed some critical ideas about organizing and the formation of organizations. He spoke about the tradeoffs like: "speculation, armchair theorizing, over determined explanations, complicated explanations" (p.41). His book lent an interesting complexity to our understanding of the formation of organizations as he was critical of trying to make understanding of organizations "general and accurate and simple". Communities were loosely knit groups (or organizations). Weick explains in important social psychological terms how to be skeptical of seeking perfection and to realize that the processes of building an organization are what is critical, recognizing the importance of "stability, continuity and repetition and similarity across time". These were things that we looked for when we tried to understand the creation of the summer institutes being created all over the United States. And these ideas resonated with what we were finding in our study of the writing project.

McLaughlin and Talbert (2001) were to write an important book on professional communities as they studied high school departments. What we learn from this book is that high school professional communities in school departments differ in their "strength and focus of mission, in locus and culture of practice – differences that matter profoundly for students and teachers alike" (p.93). Most of the high school communities they found were weak in that they were traditional and treated students in lower tracks with lower standards. But they found a few departments where teachers were colleagues, and leadership encouraged the sharing of work, discussing new ideas, developing resources, attending state and national meetings, publishing in professional journals, and even eating lunch together. Strong learning communities in high school departments had characteristics that set them apart from traditional communities:

- Teacher collaboration around problems of teaching and learning.
- A belief that all students can learn.
- High expectations for all students.
- Non-tracked classrooms.
- Focus on developing shared language and knowledge about teaching and learning.
- A commitment to active engagement and equitable achievement for all students.

What we learn is how communities are enacted in departments within the structure of a high school and the characteristics that grow when communities are successful, as well as the big hold on many departments which are traditional.

Westheimer (1998), fully aware of the tensions and difficulties of creating professional communities in schools, studied two middle schools to further clarify how these schools negotiated the pull towards autonomy on the one hand, and working together on the other hand. He was trying to understand how the processes of community-building could be more explicit and how teachers "struggle with the dilemmas of building professional communities amid competing visions" (p.29). After studying Brandeis and Mills middle schools, Westheimer offered three important lessons on professional community. He was trying to illuminate both the clarity and the complexity of communities. His three lessons include:

1. **Beliefs Matter** – In both schools it was the importance of connection and affiliation that mattered. "The content of beliefs mattered" (p.142).
2. **Structures Matter** – At Mills, most important decisions are collective, while at Brandeis decisions are not collectively made as some teachers felt that they were "not competent to make those decisions" (p.145).
3. **Individuality and Community are Unexpected Bedfellows** – Westheimer shows how individual identities are important even as teachers are working on collective efforts.

We begin to appreciate and accept the fact that researchers, policy-makers and practitioners all must recognize that there are differences in beliefs about how people work together, how they work with students, and what curriculum they espouse. And that communities will look different depending upon how they interact, participate and struggle with professional autonomy or solidarity with common agreements. Westheimer's struggle to understand all these factors becomes our struggle as well.

References

Cochran-Smith, M. & Lytle, S. (1993) *Inside/Outside: Teacher Research and Knowledge.* New York: Teachers College Press.

Gray, J. (2000) *Teachers at the Center: A Memoir of the Early Years of the National Writing Project.* Berkeley, CA: The National Writing Project.

Lieberman, A. & Wood, D.R. (2003) *Inside the National Writing Project: Connecting Network Learning and Classroom Teaching.* New York: Teachers College Press.

McLaughlin M. & Talbert, J. (2001) *Professional Communities and the Work of High School Teaching.* Chicago: University of Chicago Press.

St. John, M.M., Dickey, K., Hirabayashi, J., & Stokes, L., with assistance from Murray, A. (2001) *The National Writing Project: Client Satisfaction and Program Impact. Results from a Follow-up Survey of Participants at Summer 2000 Invitational Institutes.* Inverness, CA: Inverness Research Associates.

Weick, K. (1979) *The Social Psychology of Organizing*, 2nd edition. Philippines: Addison-Wesley.

Wenger, E. (1990) *Communities of Practice.* Cambridge: Cambridge University Press.

Westheimer, J. (1998) *Among School Teachers: Community, Autonomy and Ideology in Teachers' Work.* New York: Teachers College Press.

8

IMPROVING SCHOOLS

Understanding the dynamics
of changing practice, structure
and culture

Up until now, the book has discussed the different roles that teachers have learned to take, including as developers, researchers, scholars, leaders and participants, in a variety of reform efforts and what we have learned about how these aid school and teacher learning. What hasn't yet been discussed are the dynamics of the collective work that takes place when teachers participate in improving their practice, often changing the structure of their school and inevitably their own culture. How does this happen? What does it look like? For decades there has been research literature describing the process of change and how it takes place in schools. However, with notable exceptions, policy changes at the federal, state and local levels continue to often have questionable impact. Many have oversimplified the necessary conditions to help make school reform a reality as well as what teachers need to learn as they help to participate in building a learning community. We need to understand why this is so and how realistic reforms can be crafted and supported that include the social realities of teaching, learning and schooling (Jaquith, 2015; Lieberman, 1982).

As with the rest of this book, it is important that we understand the problems and possibilities for school improvement from the teacher's perspective (one's own classroom, the larger teacher group, and perhaps some other group that teachers belong to as, for example, has been described in Chapter 7). We start with the essential dilemma for teachers. No matter what grade level, teachers must figure out how to move the group (even as one needs to pay attention to the individuals in the class). Teachers differ dramatically in the repertoires they learn as they teach. What worked last year may be inappropriate this year. Those inside the classroom know that it is not just about having the appropriate materials, but about figuring out how to organize the class, make split-second decisions, sometimes scrap plans because they did not work, take advantage of unexpected happenings, and continue to move on. With time, teachers get better and more comfortable with the day-to-day nature of teaching and learn to handle its complexities and most often learn from them.

Moving from isolation to teacher development

Most people from the outside often do not understand the powerful effects of being in one's classroom all day, often with little interaction from other adults (Lortie, 1975). It is not hard to understand that teachers feel most comfortable in their own room because they are in control. So we have our first glitch. Most school improvement projects are aimed at the whole school, where many teachers have little experience outside their own realm.

Being cut off from other adults often makes teachers feel wary of new ideas, new curriculum, new ways of thinking such as inquiry, or starting with what students know (as opposed to what teachers know). Isolation can make teachers feel distrustful of other ideas outside of their experience as well as other people (who do not know their students). What if we think of working toward assuming and planning for teacher development in a variety of ways, working assiduously to build trust as new ideas are proposed?

> *The concept of teacher development redefines the old idea of in-service or staff development since it concerns itself with teacher's continuous inquiry into practice, viewing teachers as adult learners.*
>
> *(Lieberman and Miller, 1990)*

Building a culture of support for teacher development

We have learned over the years from both research and practice how a culture of support can be constituted. This is critical in any effort at teacher learning. The following five elements serve as important themes: building norms of collegiality, openness and trust; providing opportunities and time for disciplined inquiry; teacher learning of content in the context of their classroom; rethinking leadership roles; and forming networks, collaborations and coalitions for continuous support. These elements help build improved practice, a variety of structures to support teachers, and ways of eventually building professional cultures in schools that often change the structure of schools (Lieberman and Miller, 2008).

Developing norms of collegiality and trust

What must be considered a classic study by Judith Warren Little (1986) documents how a group of six schools built colleagueship. The principals were actively engaged with teachers and consistently provided expectations for, and modeled, behaviors of collegiality. Principals and teachers observed each other, talked about what was going on, and worked together to find solutions to problems. Privacy and isolation were replaced by shared ownership and the building of new norms for working together as well as support for inquiry. It is important to understand that these ideas of shared work and problem-solving, as well as mutual assistance and teacher leadership, formed the basis of a new and different school culture.

Rosenholtz (1989) focused her research on workplace conditions for teachers. She found that there was a strong relationship between the structures, norms and patterns of interaction that supported (or limited) teachers' growth and development. In more collaborative settings, teachers reported that teaching is a complex craft with professional learning as an unending process. In isolated settings, where there was little support from the principal, there were also barriers to collaboration, limiting the kind of professional learning that went on in the school.

Opportunities and time for disciplined inquiry

Neither elementary nor secondary schools have been structured with time for thinking and planning. But in the last few decades, a variety of methods have been described that enable teachers to actually talk together and share their pedagogical practices with one another, with time to do it outside the classroom. One idea has been a *retreat*. In this case, a full day or more away from the school has come to be accepted practice. It is here that teachers can plan together, share their practices, and decide on some collective efforts to improve areas of their practice away from the day-to-day nature of teaching.

There are some schools now that have learned to divide the work so that teachers become expert in a few areas, particularly in elementary schools. In other schools, teams have been developed and decide together a focus for their work. Other schools decide on themes for the year and work together on how they can connect to some integrating idea. These innovative structures help create opportunities for dialogue, even though time still continues to be a problem for all.

Teacher learning of content in the context of teaching

Teacher learning and student learning can be seen as sharing a common developmental idea. Viewed from this perspective, all learners have developing abilities. The problem for the teacher and the school then is to match learning opportunities to these developing abilities. Recent research on cognition supports this developmentalist view. This research recognizes the complexity of learning in school: the necessity for some time to be organized for students to construct problems that may be poorly defined so they can learn from their mistakes; and learn the importance of the mix of social and cognitive skills that help define problems (Devaney and Sykes, 1988). Teaching and learning are not seen as separate functions. Teachers are learners too. They pose questions, help solve problems in their own practice, and can think deeply about understanding the learning process for themselves *and* their students.

Rethinking leadership, learning and community in schools

For the past fifty years, many people have written about the functions of leadership and a whole new view of leadership has been proposed. Up until the present time, some researchers have taken on the bureaucratic-hierarchical nature of schools and worked on the conflicts that accrue when the collegial nature of reform is tried.

Wenger (1998, p.4) posited the idea that learning comes about based on a different set of assumptions. He introduced the idea of *social learning*, which includes *practice* (talking about what you do), *meaning* (learning as intentional), *community* (learning as participating and being with others), and *identity* (learning as changing who we are).

This kind of thinking and learning has helped change the very discussion of leadership and the building of community as essentials in schools. In its earliest phases, Cochran-Smith and Lytle (1999) wrote about the different conceptions of teacher learning (knowledge *for* practice, knowledge *in* practice and knowledge *of* practice), which included knowledge on dissemination, practical knowledge and systematic inquiry in communities. At the same time, Little (1986) described the move from the independence of teachers to *interdependence*, analyzing the conditions under which teachers really do act as colleagues. She introduced the ideas that teachers give *assistance*, *share materials*, and even do *joint work* (such as on an interdisciplinary team). Her analysis at this time taught many of us that learning and leadership in authentic professional communities was rare, on the one hand, yet powerful in changing the norms of privacy on the other.

The growth of teacher leadership

In the early 2000s, researchers began to write about *teacher leadership* within the context of professional learning communities both inside and outside schools, thus joining two important ideas that demanded changes not just in roles and responsibilities, but in learning how to go public with teaching, learning to collaborate, and learning to lead from the teacher's perspective. These new responsibilities demanded changes in practice and structure, and eventually changes in the culture of the school.

Those who become teacher leaders learn quickly that teachers need to develop their capacity to talk honestly about their practice; learn to do knowledge work; go public with their work; and eventually connect their professional learning to their classroom practice and student learning (Lieberman and Miller, 2008, p.23).

Building the capacity for honest talk

Teachers know that there is a difference between congeniality and collegiality. Congeniality is where people are nice and amiable, but actually avoid anything that might bring on a conflict of ideas. Collegiality, on the other hand, is where teachers develop bonds of trust and learn to reflect on and provide honest feedback even when there is disagreement. Collegial groups stand in great contrast to most traditional school cultures that value individualism, isolation and privacy.

The capacity to do knowledge work

For most teachers initially, theory and research are considered irrelevant to their teaching. Experience is what matters (not theory). Schön (1983) first introduced the idea that professionals need a more adequate way of describing how they learn and think about their craft. He proposed the idea that "reflection in action" is a form of "thinking on your feet". By looking at their own behaviors and responses to a situation, a teacher can generate new understandings and, in fact, learn from them. Schön referred to this as "theory-in-use", the idea that reflective practice leads to learning that can be practical, active and open to revision. These ideas went a long way to helping to conceptualize how teachers think, act and learn.

The capacity to go public

Teachers who eventually get connected to some form of a community, whether inside the school, or outside, learn to talk about their successes and their failures with their colleagues. We saw this kind of talk in those who were at the summer institute run by the NWP. As we noted:

> *After a teacher reads a paper aloud in the "author's chair", colleagues provide feedback. This feedback, in turn informs subsequent revisions, and then revisions are shared. As drafts improve over time, fellows see for themselves how public presentation has the power to motivate and produce high quality work.*
>
> (Lieberman and Wood, 2002, p. 17)

When the ideas and strategies poured out, we saw an ethic of privacy give way to an ethic of "swapping ideas".

As Cochran-Smith and Lytle (1993) have noted, in Philadelphia teacher research communities construct oral or written texts that are disseminated to group members and externally to a wider group. These texts include journals, oral inquiries, classroom and school studies. This is another way of going public with one's work. Some of these appear in *Inside/Outside: Teacher Research and Knowledge* (1993).

Reflecting on the themes of: Context, capacity, challenge and culture

School contexts differ significantly. Where a community is located, the culture that surrounds it, the way it gets started and how teachers and principals relate to one another all matter. Different contexts present different demands and require different strategies for principals and teachers. For some, a starting point is taking an idea and figuring out together how to think about and perhaps use the idea. For others, it is about how to build trust so that teachers can learn to talk with each other about their practice – what works and what doesn't. Or it is about creating a new context where teachers can go public with their work, learn to discuss their teaching and create a learning community together. All of these ideas share the fact that teachers and principals need to develop the capacity to step out of their isolation and find and develop a commitment to work as a community. As commitments develop, so do the connections teachers make to each other and their collective concerns about improving their practice. Content knowledge needs to develop as it is matched with a sense of community and connects to the needs of the teachers and their students (as well as to their principal).

We know that no changes in culture come without challenge. Schools are not any different. How do you build trust when you have always worked alone? How, and in what ways, do schools develop "learning" communities that honor where teachers start (isolated) and what they can accomplish with others (a community) that helps sustain and support learning? Where do you start? How do you connect personal and intellectual concerns with some kind of content? How do teachers learn to share the leadership responsibilities for changing the norms of schools from isolation to the building of a learning community?

The trend toward building professional learning communities rooted in real teacher practice that involves new ways of interacting with colleagues, joining competence and community and connecting intellectual as well as the social needs of educators, holds tremendous promise for engaging teachers as learners as well as leaders.

See: *Teachers in Professional Communities: Improving Teaching and Learning* (2008) by Lieberman and Miller. Portions from this publication have been used in this chapter.

Expanding our knowledge

In a recently published book, Jaquith (2017) has written about and explained what the conditions for learning are and how to help create them. Rather than focusing on one thing at a time, she has helped to create and explain how different conditions fit together to influence the process of growing and supporting teacher and student learning. She focuses on building instructional capacity (ICB), which she writes is a "practical theory". We learn that there are four types of instructional resources, and to provide for continuous learning all of these need to be developed in some way. The four types of instructional resources are:

• **Instructional knowledge**
  Expertise in: content, pedagogy, content knowledge, local context

- **Instructional technology**
  Methods, routines, tools, materials
- **Instructional relationships**
  Trust, respect, integrity, psychological safety, recognition of others' expertise
- **Organizational resources**
  Structures, leadership positions, organizational routines, norms for discussion.
  (Jacquith, 2017, p.16)

Because the instructional resources are complex within themselves, Jaquith describes developing the capacity to use instructional resources as a cycle. This helps explain how creating the conditions for learning "requires coordinated action and interdependence across people who do the work of improving teaching and student learning" (Jaquith, 2017, p.167). And it helps us understand why many attempts at improving practice falter. It becomes clear that a collaborative approach to learning is essential if the kinds of resources are to be not only available, but supported at different levels of the system.

What do we know so far about how to develop and support the instructional resources that Jaquith describes? First, we have to start with a problem to be solved that relates to improving student learning: organize all the instructional resources available; mobilize for interdependent work; and create opportunities for action that can improve workplace conditions. And at the same time, keep support, discussion, creativity and continuous improvement efforts going.

As we know, the process of change is rarely smooth and without tension or even conflict. But Jaquith has seriously deepened our understanding of the idea that all these resources are involved in improving education. They must be organized; and time must be spent engaging people, and supporting the necessary actions and interactions along the way. This all takes time, effort, leadership and continuous opportunities if successful change is to be accomplished.

The growth of professional learning communities

In the last two decades there has been much activity and some research into how schools are developing professional learning communities that can change the isolation many teachers feel into collaboration with colleagues. Putting teachers at the helm in building these communities has become an international phenomenom (Harris, Jones and Huffman, 2018).

Harris, Jones and Huffman support the idea described in several chapters of this book, that too often teachers are assumed to be passive recipients of reform mandated by policymakers distant from the complexities of practice. They further suggest that much of school reform fails as reformers often do not understand that teachers' views are critical to the reform process. Harris, Jones and Huffman also suggest that teachers need to be central and lead the process of school improvement. Earlier, Lieberman and Miller (2008, p.1) wrote that the "real life of school, with its inherent contradictions, ongoing routines, and unrelenting dailiness often intervenes; and the best of intentions fail to materialize as planned". They asked: Why do so many policies that are based on the best research available fail to deliver? Why aren't programs that focus on improvements in content knowledge and teaching techniques enough?

These questions are answered by coming to understand how different countries all over the world have realized that teachers leading professional learning communities make the difference (Harris, Jones and Huffman, 2018). Teachers are central, not peripheral; teachers lead and learn together. We learn that there are different ways of forming professional learning communities, different ways of building support structures and trusting relationships, and important ways that teachers are *leading* school, district and sometimes system, improvement. Harris's edited book documents countries all over the world.

In Ontario, teachers write a proposal to do school improvement, get financed, and lead the organization of teacher development (Campbell, Lieberman and Yashkina, 2016). In the process of developing a team effort, teachers also learn to take leadership in the process. Ten years of research evidence has backed up this claim and made school improvement led by teachers successful.

In England, studying three different projects, Stoll et al. focused on the power of "middle leaders" as change catalysts. They found that the most successful leaders had "drive and energy, stimulated meaningful informal conversations to connect and support development"

(2018, p.56). They role modeled, involved others, and kept up the morale. These leaders supported and coached their colleagues and helped to develop trusting relationships with professional learning teams.

In Taiwan, Peiying Chen writes about how networked learning communities created important learning opportunities as they experimented with learner-centered pedagogy. The chapter describes how teachers opened up a "bottom-up" approach to change and the impact that this had on the whole system (that was used to top-down approaches).

Professional learning communities from Singapore, Scotland, Wales, New Zealand, China and England help us understand the leadership roles of teachers, and the different ways in which learning communities are built in different cultures. We learn more about teacher leadership and collaboration by looking at cross-cultural examples of what it takes to create an interface between policy and practice.

References

Baker-Doyle, K. (2011) *The Networked Teacher: How New Teachers Build Social Networks for Professional Support*. New York: Teachers College Press.

Campbell, C., Lieberman, A., & Yashkina, A. (2016) Developing professional capital in policy and practice: Ontario's teacher learning and leadership program. *Journal of Professional Capital and Community*, 1(3), 219–236.

Cochran-Smith, M. & Lytle, S. (1999) Teacher learning in communities. *Review of Research in Education*, 24, 249–306.

Cochran-Smith, M. & Lytle, S. (1993) *Inside/Outside: Teacher Research and Knowledge*. New York: Teachers College Press.

Devaney, K. & Sykes, G. (1988) Making the case for professionalism. In Lieberman, A. (Ed.), *Building a Professional Culture in Schools*. New York: Teachers College Press, pp. 3–22.

Harris, A., Jones, M., & Huffman, J.B. (Eds.) (2018) *Teachers Leading Educational Reform: The Power of Professional Communities*. Abingdon, Oxon: Routledge.

Jaquith, A. (2015) Site-based leadership for improving instruction. *Educational Forum*, 79(1), 12–23.

Jaquith, A. (2017) *How to Create the Conditions for Learning: Continuous Improvement in Classrooms, Schools, and Districts*. Cambridge, MA: Harvard Education Press.

Lieberman, A. (1982) *Practice Makes Policy: The Tensions of School Improvement in Policy Making in Education*. Chicago: The National Society for the Study of Education.

Lieberman, A. & Miller, L. (1990) Teacher development in professional practice schools. *Teachers College Record*, 92(1), 105–122.

Lieberman, A. & Wood, D.R. (2002) *Inside the National Writing Project: Connection Network Learning and Classroom Teaching*. New York: Teachers College Press.

Lieberman, A. & Miller, L. (2008) *Teachers in Professional Communities: Improving Teaching and Learning*. New York: Teachers College Press.

Lieberman, A., Campbell, C., & Yashkina, A. (2017) *Teacher Learning and Leadership, Of, By, and For Teachers*. New York: Routledge.

Little, J.W. (1986) Seductive images and organizational realities in professional development. In Lieberman, A. (Ed.), *Rethinking School Improvement: Research, Craft and Concept*. New York: Teachers College Press, pp. 26–44.

Lortie, D. (1975) *Schoolteacher: A Sociological Study*. Chicago: University of Chicago Press.

Rosenholtz, S. (1989) *Teachers' Workplace*. New York: Longman, Inc.

Schön, D.A. (1983) *The Reflective Practitioner*. New York: Basic Books.

Stoll, L., Brown, C., Spence-Thomas, K., & Taylor, C. (2018) Teacher leadership within and across professional learning communities. In Harris, A., Jones, M., & Huffman, J.B. (Eds.), *Teachers Leading Educational Reform: The Power of Professional Learning*. Abingdon, Oxon: Routledge, pp. 51–71.

Wenger, E. (1998) *Communities of Practice: Learning, Meaning and Identity*. Cambridge: Cambridge University Press.

9

TEACHERS AT THE HELM

Learning and leading

In 2003, there was a critical election in Ontario, Canada where the politics and parties shifted, from the conservatives to the liberals. The election was critical for teachers and schools as the conservatives had mandated that all teachers take a number of courses, which was almost universally unpopular, while the liberals wanted to work *with* teachers in some kind of collaborative arrangement. The liberals won!

What actually happened was that over a two-year period the Ontario Teacher's Federation (OTF) and representatives from the Ministry of Education met together and created a program entitled the *Teacher Learning and Leadership Program* (TLLP). They not only invented a program together, but created an important opportunity for *teachers to decide* (with their colleagues) what the school needed, what *teachers* could learn about improvements in their practice, and at the same time how they could develop as leaders in their school. And each proposal if accepted came with a budget!

In a real sense, this was *creating the conditions for teacher learning and leadership* (rather than telling teachers what to do to improve).

The purposes and processes of TLLP

I have been with the program as a keynote speaker since the beginning; it is now in its tenth year. I later became a member of the research group. In 2007 it began in Toronto as a joint initiative between the Ontario Ministry of Education and the OTF. The program has three purposes:

- To support experienced teachers to undertake advanced professional development.
- To develop teachers' leadership skills for sharing their professional learning and exemplary practices.
- To facilitate knowledge exchange for the spread and sustainability of effective and innovative practices.

This collaborative program encourages each Board to support teachers who write a proposal to conduct professional development in their own school. In the proposal, teachers include a description of the proposed project, how the project will contribute to student learning, and Ontario's priorities for educational excellence, equity, wellbeing, and public confidence. A plan including specific goals, activities, measures and budget is submitted.

Successful applicants come to a conference where there are workshops on how to understand how to use a budget, how to introduce the project, meet with other teachers, and join the TLLP community. The conference is entitled *Leadership Skills for Classroom Teachers*. The conference supports teacher preparation to take on professional learning, project management and leadership expectations of a TLLP project – which lasts for eighteen months. Each Board can have at least two projects each year. In this way, the TLLP has spread across Ontario, and has been supporting teachers and their proposals since 2007.

Creating a learning community

During their TLLP project, participants become part of *Mentoring Moments*, an online community for sharing resources, learning and discussion. In this way, teachers feel supported from the start, during, and even after the project is over. In November of the following year there is a second conference (*Sharing the Learning Summit*) where the teachers come and set up their work that they have developed so that it can be shared with other teachers. Typically, a TLLP project spans eighteen months from initial training, through implementation, and then to the culminating summit. What this does is it supports teachers and their colleagues from the beginning to the end of their project and they naturally form a community of learners that now number in the thousands (as 85% work with a team). The actual number of TLLP projects numbers about 1,000 since its beginning.

In the process of writing a successful proposal, teachers have an opportunity to learn leadership skills such as: learning to build a team; sharing leadership responsibilities; finding out what their leadership strengths are; and how to implement a professional development effort with teachers as leaders, rather than objects of other people's research.

Designing research on TLLP

Sometime during the second year of the program, we suggested to the collaborative that they let us do research on the TLLP. It appeared to us to be very successful and was beginning to show how this radical idea of providing the opportunities to learn and lead seemed to be very powerful where teachers, rather than outsiders, were both the learners and the leaders of professional development. It seemed like the perfect moment to document how, and in what ways, the program was realizing its purposes and its potential as well as what might be problematic.

We were sponsored for a beginning piece of research as well as three others which came later. The collaborative of the government and the OTF saw the power of actually documenting the various practices that were taken up by the TLLP, how teachers learned along the way, and how the very process of *doing* and *sharing* the work with other colleagues taught them the processes of *learning leadership*.

Collecting evidence from research

Our first research project was a small-scale, one-year project looking at the benefits and challenges of the TLLP. We sampled 60 final reports from 2007 to 2011. Our questions were:

- What is the value of the TLLP for teachers?
- To what extent have the goals of the TLLP been realized?
- What lessons have been learned so far?

Our methods included: analysis of TLLP documents; observations and evaluations of provincial events for TLLP participants; analysis of a sample of final reports; an in-depth analysis of a sample of sixty projects (out of 302); and interviews with individuals, including project teacher leaders, teacher union leaders and government officials. We learned that the most prevalent TLLP project topics were:

1. Differentiated instruction
2. Literacy
3. Technology
4. Professional learning communities

Following the reportage of the first study, we were invited to do three additional studies. The first study included projects from 2007 to 2011. The second study included the projects from the next few years (2013–2014), while the third study documented 2014 to 2015. The fourth study will be a summary of what we have learned so far (in progress).

The second study (2013–2014)

In the second study, we asked three different questions:

1. What is the impact of TLLP projects for:

- Teacher's professional learning?
- Teachers' knowledge and skills?

- Other adults affected by the TLLP?
- Student engagement and learning?

2. How is learning being shared beyond the TLLP team?

- What approaches to sharing learning are being used?
- How does sharing of learning affect participants?
- What approaches appear to support the spread of knowledge and changes in practice?

3. What longer-term impact from participating in TLLP can be identified for TLLP leaders, project team members, schools, districts and other participants?

We found that the following had an incredibly strong impact: organizing a collaborative learning group; providing professional dialogue, and self-reflection as well as action research carried out on networking, co-teaching, planning and more (Campbell, Lieberman and Yashkina, 2015). And we were able to obtain some important information on how teachers "learned leadership". We got ten people to write about what they did, who they did it with, what they learned and what they learned about leadership.

Learning leadership

People wrote about their peers, partners and teams, and how they learned to build a team, figured out how to share leadership and support people when they had problems, and, most importantly, what they learned about their own strengths and weaknesses as leaders. Each of the ten people wrote vignettes that ranged from three to ten pages in length.

In all cases, people learned three big ideas concerning leadership: collaboration, courage and support. They described how they learned to share, be open about their practice and to extend leadership to other team members. Interestingly, all ten people who wrote vignettes wrote about going to research first for ideas and other sources of expertise in order to develop their own knowledge. For them, leadership meant building their own capacity to learn new knowledge and skills as well as how to work with and learn from one another. This did not mean that there were no challenges; there were. Sometimes it was working with difficult others, sometimes it was their own failings as a leader, sometimes it was not recognizing that teachers needed to be heard.

> *People don't want to follow (so you need to feel good about how you lead.)*
> *It is challenging to organize a large group of teachers!*
> *Sometimes it is hard to remember that people need to feel that they are heard.*

What we were beginning to understand was that for teachers, learning leadership was *personal, problematic, powerful and potentially influential* (Campbell, Lieberman and Yashkina, 2014–2015). As teachers began to organize their peers and work to move the work along and see professional development in the context of teaching, they were learning that starting with the teacher and how they learned to work with others was a powerful way of including the complexities of teaching as teachers live it daily, learning along the way and becoming someone who could also take on leadership (and learn how to do it).

> *TLLP has been one of the best learning experiences that the school community and I have participated in. Teachers need time to collaborate, co-teach, debrief and learn together.*
> *This has been one of the most empowered experiences of my career!*

Many teachers claimed that they learned how to communicate with others – sometimes for the first time. They learned how to plan, use their time, look at new ideas and felt that teacher-friendly professional development could be powerful.

They learned a lot of things in the process of the work. How do you keep people involved? How do you use others' strengths? How do you build collective ideas so that people feel important, trusted and respected for their contributions? Many learned how complicated it was to collaborate. And many learned how powerful it was to grow their leadership potential.

Writing vignettes about leadership

In each of our studies, we had teachers writing vignettes. We assumed that this would be one way of possibly gaining a deeper understanding of the "processes of learning leadership". As described in Chapter 4, we always provided teachers with prompts so they would not have to worry about creating great stories of their leadership. They could answer the prompts and a narrative would provide the processes of how they learned leadership in their project. This turned out to be important information for our studies of TLLP. In our 2013–2014 study, we had nineteen people who wrote vignettes. Of the nineteen, eight worked on a team, seven worked with one colleague, and four worked on their own. Most of the teachers worked with someone else and in doing so changed not only *what* they were doing, but *how* they learned to work together.

> *I have experienced how to manage conflict of opinions, budgeting, release time, and how to navigate issues within the changing school environment.*
>
> *I feel that I have gained valuable experience dealing with keeping my colleagues moving forward on a project with time and budget restraints, while maintaining a strong working relationship based on respect, trust, and acknowledgements of each other's contributions.*
>
> *(Campbell, Lieberman and Yashkina, April 2014)*

The vignettes turned out to provide a lot of examples and stories of how teachers *learned* to work together, how they could all contribute to a collective need for professional development, and, in the process, many learned that they could facilitate learning in others through their newfound learning of leadership. TLLP has turned out to be an incredible source of knowledge as well as an outstanding way of implementing professional development as teachers learn how to lead collectively.

We will have done four different research studies of the TLLP, clearly showing the power and progress of teachers being the initiators of organizing professional development. And we clearly saw the opportunities for teachers to learn leadership along the way – sometimes leading to other leadership opportunities, and sometimes teaching teachers the power of facilitating leadership themselves (or for others). In 2017 we published a book entitled: *Teacher Learning and Leadership: Of, By, and For Teachers* (Lieberman, Campbell and Yashkina).

Expanding our knowledge

Earlier, Hargreaves had written about the fact that "how teachers worked with their students affects how they work with teachers". He moved the conversation to talking about changing the "culture of teaching" as the big idea (Hargreaves, 1997). He further developed the idea that teachers needed to learn ways of collaborating with one another, although he was, in the best of ways, also teaching us the difficulty of doing this.

In addition to his writing on building a culture of teaching, Hargreaves wrote importantly about the emotional dimensions of teaching, which were critically important to understanding how asking teachers to change the way they teach, the way they assess their students, and the way they map backward to identify the methods and materials they need for particular outcomes, has not only an educational dimension, but an emotional one as well. He was one of the first to recognize and write about the importance of connecting emotions to the problems of changing and improving one's teaching, a critical idea which had been absent from the discussions of school and teacher change.

Hargreaves and Shirley (2009) brought together government policy, professional involvement and public engagement – releasing teachers from control and engaging readers in a view that that connects teacher professionalism to a view of collaboration with government involvement and support. They describe in important detail what it will take to create coherence in education. They include four catalysts that are significant:

- Sustainable leadership
- Integrating networks
- Responsibility before accountability
- Differentiation and diversity

In an outstnding analysis of the four catalysts and their importance, Hargreaves and Shirley end with what they mean by the "Fourth Way", the title of the book: "It is a democratic and professional path to improvement that builds from the bottom, steers from the top, and provides support and pressure from the sides" (p.107).

In the last several decades, it has become more obvious to many that even the words concerning learning have changed. Staff development became professional development and for some even professional learning. Several authors wrote about the fact that strategies for teacher learning can be very different. New ways of thinking about professional development began to appear. People wrote about the fact that there were huge differences in the way in which teachers are approached and involved. The different views included:

- Compliance vs. Capacity building
- Bureaucratic vs. Professional orientation
- Direct teaching vs. Growth in practice
- Individual vs. Collaborative
- High stakes accountability vs. Building trust in teachers
  (Lieberman, Campbell and Yashkina, 2017, p.13)

One of the most important studies produced by two researchers was a book on *professional communities* (McLaughlin and Talbert, 2001). In studying high school departments, McLaughlin and Talbert began to write about "communities of practice" and how they differed. In some communities, "teachers are mutually engaged in teaching; they jointly develop their practice; and they share a repertoire of resources and history" (p.41). They found other communities where teachers had "deficit views of non-traditional students", while others shared a belief that "all students can meet high academic standards". Their research began to flesh out what is meant by professional communities and how it defined the way in which teachers believed in and taught their students. It began to deepen our understanding of what is meant by community and why it was such an important, yet complex, idea.

Westheimer (1998) studied two middle schools – Brandeis and Mills – as teacher communities. In his brilliant book, he analyzes the difficulties and subtleties of what is meant by a professional community. By looking at both the conceptual literature and a series of reports supporting changes in schools (e.g. *A Nation Prepared, Tomorrow's Teachers*, etc.), he documents the characteristics of professional communities (interaction and participation, interdependence, shared interests and beliefs, concern for individuals, minority views, and meaningful relationships). To gain a greater depth of understanding of the organizational conditions that contribute to the development of communities, he studied two middle schools (Brandeis and Mills).

What he found in studying these two well-respected schools was that they had huge differences in goals, structures, processes and beliefs – yet both regarded themselves as professional communities. His contribution was significant as it exposed the differences in two schools that had their own definitions of shared beliefs (Brandeis believed the purpose of schooling was to provide a challenging learning environment that fosters independence and personal responsibility – and the purpose of Mills was to have students live and work in a world that is characterized by independence and cultural diversity) (Westheimer, 1998, p.122). So too did they differ on how they participated, built interdependence, and built relationships. Westheimer was to open up the complexities of building community and deepened our understanding of learning, leadership and participation.

TLLP turns out to be an extraordinary example of how teachers learn and learn to lead when they have the power and possibilities for organizing the learning with their peers. We now have the evidence from others as well as our studies of the ten years of the TLLP to show the positive results of professional learning and the growth of leadership when teachers are at the helm and are supported both technically and organizationally by the collaboration of policymakers and the teachers' federation.

References

Campbell, C., Lieberman, A., & Yashkina, A. (2013, 2014, 2015) *Teacher Learning and Leadership Program: Research Reports.* Ontario Teachers Federation.

Hargreaves, A. (Ed.). (1997) *Rethinking Educational Change with Heart and Mind.* Alexandria, VA: Association for Supervision and Curriculum Development, 1997 Yearbook.

Hargreaves, A. & Shirley, D. (2009) *The Fourth Way: The Inspiring Future for Educational Change.* A joint publication by Corwin, Ontario Principal's Council and National Staff Development Council.

Lieberman, A., Campbell, C., & Yashkina, A. (2017) *Teacher Learning and Leadership: Of, By, and For Teachers.* London and New York: Routledge.

McLaughlin, M.W. & Talbert, J.E. (2001) *Professional Communities and the Work of High School Teaching.* Chicago: University of Chicago Press.

Westheimer, J. (1998) *Among Schoolteachers: Community, Autonomy, and Ideology in Teachers' Work.* New York: Teachers College Press.

10

A SOCIAL VIEW OF TEACHING, LEARNING AND LEADING

From isolation to collaboration and community

It has been over fifty years since I was teaching my sixth grade class in Simi Valley, California. Much has changed and we have learned many lessons, from experience, research, history, technology, and the continuous changing nature of the world as well as education.

This book, along with my experience, and that of many other researchers in the field, can now speak of several big ideas that appear to be important in improving schooling for both principals, teachers and their students. They include:

- Teacher Learning
- Teacher Leadership
- Teachers as Scholars
- Learning Communities
- Connecting Research with Practice

Teacher learning

Even though I was a teacher in June and then on a school university project in September as a doctoral student in the 1960s, I realized that the possibilities for continuous teacher learning was not necessarily a natural part of being a teacher in a school. Isolation was the norm for most teachers, which limited what they might learn and prevented them from learning with and from others. I was responsible for working with two schools in the *League of Cooperating Schools* (LCS) project in 1966, and we had to learn to find the time, the right strategies for working together, how to talk and behave as an outsider, and the necessary organizational supports for teachers to try new things in their classroom. Principals had to be willing to support teacher learning and help find the time, the reasons, the importance and the willingness for it to happen. Being in the LCS helped support the principals (as the big idea was that principals were the key agents of change), but what about the teachers? We were to find out that it was more complicated than only supporting principals. There was much to learn about how to engage teachers in improving their learning, either with (or without) the actual support of the principals. It was fine to say that the principals were the "key agents of change", but what about the teachers who were supposed to change their classroom work and "individualize instruction"? How were the principals to "facilitate" teacher learning? What would this entail as a principal (or a teacher)? Who was to deal with conflict? Time? Engagement? What kind of learning was necessary for principals to facilitate how to engage teachers, provide them with time to learn, and help support them in creating a culture in the school that encouraged continuous learning as a natural part of their work?

Teachers on a team with researchers

Even when we loaded the deck with teachers (see Chapter 2) by putting five teachers on a team with a researcher and a staff developer, teachers were not comfortable enough to see themselves as equal partners to researchers. We realized, after the fact, that teachers had to learn what research was, how they could be involved in it, and why it could be important to them. We had three teams, but only the team at Scarsdale was successful in providing important opportunities for teacher learning. But they had worked for many years at recognizing that teachers were the best teachers of each other and their learning. (The professional development of teachers was run by teachers learning lessons from their peers.) A team at Scarsdale was made up of teachers who had an equal voice to any other members of the team.

Tom Sobol, who was the superintendent of Scarsdale at the time, realized that teachers could not only be leaders, but that they were the best professional developers of teachers too. This district, under his leadership, was an outstanding example of teacher learning, leadership and community building, but it had come from the leadership at the district level and the innovative work of the superintendent and the district, as well as the teacher's union. And it had taken years to learn how to work together, what structures were needed to engage teachers, and how collaboration between teachers, principals and district leadership could really make positive changes possible.

Teachers as leaders

It took many years before it was recognized by some districts that teachers could be leaders. For me and Diane Wood, who did a study of the National Writing Project (NWP) (Lieberman and Wood, 2003), we learned that teachers coming to a summer institute (which ran from three to five weeks during the summer) provided the first instance for us showing that when you created the opportunities for teachers to learn, teachers could also learn to lead. At the institute, teachers wrote, taught their best lessons, and learned to read and critique research. The trick then was for them to have principals who would not feel threatened that teachers could also lead in their school. Teachers were learning by using their own experience as teachers first, before they read or learned from others. This was a huge insight that the NWP introduced to the world! Much of the leadership at the time was expected from the principal. This was a radical change that the writing project understood, but was not universally accepted by others in education. It was a big departure from thinking about leadership solely by the principal, to believing that teachers could be leaders as well, without usurping the role of the principal. The writing project showed that learning leadership for teachers was a process of involving others, sharing learning, struggling together about ideas for teaching, and supporting each other in the process.

Teachers as scholars

When Lee Shulman became the head of the Carnegie Foundation for the Advancement of Teaching, he introduced the idea that both those in higher education and teachers could be scholars. The search for what this meant encouraged not only teacher learning, but leadership, collaboration and the idea that teachers could share an equal place with researchers in learning, leadership and the building of community. These ideas took decades to become accepted by educators as it meant that teachers could be scholars just like researchers – and that great teachers could teach us all how to understand the complexities of teaching and learning! (see Chapter 5). These ideas developed over the course of many years at Carnegie with the help of several cohorts of teachers and teacher educators as we worked on scholarship and what it could mean for teachers.

The advent of technology, as well as the knowledge of one of our team (Desiree Pointer Mace), helped us understand how you could both *tell* some of the lessons of scholarship and *show* other lessons, with the sum total approaching "scholarship". In this way, you could enrich showing the complexities of teaching by using the web. This was incredible learning for all of us at Carnegie as well as the teachers and teacher educators who worked with us. We were not only learning about technology, but how it could display the complicated idea of teaching in all its complexities (see insideteaching.org).

Creating the conditions for learning

Diane Wood and I were fortunate that in the 1990s we studied the NWP by looking carefully at two sites in the United States. I took UCLA in Los Angeles as it was an old site and I had gone to UCLA and lived in LA. It was an older site of the NWP. Diane took Oklahoma as it was a relatively new site. In this way, we thought we could get a sense of what was going on during the summer institute (the main way teachers got introduced to the NWP) and we could see whether the strategies were consistent – whether the site was old or new. We each went to the summer institute every day looking for the routines, organizing structures and strategies that seemed to involve teachers.

We realized that the key was that the "work" was what teachers taught in their own classrooms and their own writing about topics of their choice as they experienced the process of writing themselves.

It was not about teachers learning something from the outside, but learning to deepen their understanding of their own teaching practice as they did it every day as insiders. This was a big and important idea! It meant that opening up teachers to new learning could start by having them share what they did in their own classrooms first (before they looked to research or other teachers). It also meant that teachers who taught their best lessons were providing other teachers with ideas, strategies and ways of learning that had worked for them. This way of learning for teachers was a radical departure from learning from the professional developer who would come to your school. It meant that you could learn from other teachers, learn how to connect to others, and you could begin to learn the skills and abilities of how to belong to a learning community.

Teachers as learners and leaders

From 2007 until the present time, the program named the Teacher Learning and Leadership Program (TLLP) has come full circle in recognizing not only that teachers can learn, as in the NWP, but that they can be the center of learning and leadership in their schools and beyond (see Chapter 7). Starting from a collaboration between the government (policy makers) and the Ontario Teachers Federation (OTF) (the representative of four teacher unions), TLLP became a collaborative program that linked policy with practice for the first time in my experience. What this did was provide immediate support for teachers to learn new ideas as this was professional development for the school, as well as providing opportunities for teachers to learn to lead. It also meant that those who wrote proposals could be supported financially in their work, providing opportunities for teachers to improve their work in their school and for the proposer to learn leadership during the process of helping organize improvement efforts in their school. It also meant that whatever was learned in a particular school could be shared beyond their school.

I have been involved with this program since its inception (ten years). I have seen it become embedded in the work of Ontario, spreading the idea that teachers can be the ones to improve their schools and that they can share what they learn with others, facilitated by their principal. During the process, teachers learn how to negotiate the provisions for organizing professional development, continuous learning and working collaboratively.

For me, this was an incredible program that fitted in with my lifetime struggle of fighting for teachers' representation in improving their teaching, having equal rights with researchers, and not minimizing the complexities of teaching practice. For many it also meant building the conditions for community with both researchers and teachers. It has taken over fifty years for us all to begin to understand how this could come about, how collaboration could be built, and how teachers could be at the forefront in leading school improvement and developing a professional culture in their school and beyond. These ideas of putting teachers in charge of professional development helped formulate and provide the conditions for teacher learning as well as helping principals learn how to "facilitate" this learning as part of the role of being a principal. This program is ten years old!

Expanding our knowledge

Karl Weick's (1979) important book, *The Social Psychology of Organizing*, where he explains that "action precedes goals" and writes that much organizational research is "general and accurate and simple" (p.41) opened people up to embracing the complexities of organizing and what that might mean. He explains that research is much more complicated, involving "people, money, time, solutions, problems, and choices" (p.42). This kind of thinking opened up ideas about other features of organizations that had yet to be discussed, as educators began to talk about such terms as collaborations, learning communities, continuous professional learning, etc. These ideas were important descriptions of what was happening in the TLLP, both the successes and the struggles (see, Lieberman, Campbell and Yashkina, 2017).

Although Wenger's (1998) book was published several decades after Weick's, he introduced the idea that there is such a thing as a "social theory of learning". He deepened our understanding of learning, which we had all accepted as an individual process, and wrote about the fact that learning is fundamentally a social phenomenon. For many of us this was a very important idea. For Wenger, a social theory of learning consisted of four different components:

1. Meaning – a way of talking about our changing ability.
2. Practice – a way of sustaining engagement in action.
3. Community – a way of talking about the social configurations of participation.
4. Identity – a way of talking about how learning changes who we are and how we work in the context of our communities.

These ideas became known as "communities of practice". It was a different way of talking about engagement and seemed to fit in with our growing understanding of how teachers learned from one another and how, in the process, they helped grow a different culture in their school – a communal, rather than an individual, culture.

This view was an important predecessor to the educational community enlarging their view of what became *professional learning, learning communities,* and *building collaborative activities.* It helped us better understand why building a community in a school could supplant the isolation that many teachers feel. Although it took many years, it helped explain the continuous efforts to create learning communities in schools.

Needless to say, researchers now began to look critically at professional learning communities (Talbert, 2010) as the idea became so popular that there was the assumption that anyone could do it. What research has taught us is that there are many challenges in building these communities as they are actually an attempt to change the professional culture of a school from one led bureaucratically to one functioning professionally. Talbert calls our attention to the central idea that there are bureaucratic and professional strategies for change. Bureaucratic patterns such as mandating collaboration from the top down can only create compliance and resistance. Professional approaches demand the organizing of a shared vision, learning from one another and developing the kind of resources needed to learn this new way of working. It takes time to build a collaborative, shared process even as new resources are created. Pressure and conflict are inevitable as the changes that are needed in developing a professional culture are often the opposite to how schools are usually run bureaucratically.

Sahlberg (2010) has long written about schooling in Finland as an example of the kind of professional reform principles that have been developed over time as they have moved to a professional orientation of teaching and learning. He documents the changes that have occurred in the society from the 1970s until the present day and how they have encouraged changes in the school system. Rather than featuring standardization, they have created the following typical conditions in schools:

1. Confidence in teachers and principals as professionals.
2. Encouraging teachers to be innovative.
3. Featuring creativity while respecting learning.

The need for sophisticated knowledge and skills has provided the Finnish educational system with this radical renewal focusing on an information society and a knowledge economy (p.340). These changes have made Finland a model educational nation with enormous success, quite the opposite of many countries still adhering to a bureaucratic orientation and organization.

As Hargreaves (2010) reminds us, "high-performance is associated with highly qualified teachers being accorded wide professional flexibility for curriculum and pedagogical decisions within broad boundaries . . ." (p.106). This turns out to be a good description of the pedagogy and learning in Finland. After studying what is going on there, Hargreaves noted that Finland has a strong system of support and investment that is funded by high taxes, and attracts a high caliber of people as teachers. This social support and public investment in schools and teachers also comes with a high level of trust.

Connecting research with practice

As a keynote speaker for the TLLP in 2007 and 2008 in Toronto, Canada, I realized that the government and the OTF had created something new and important (see Chapter 7). Teachers were in charge of organizing professional development in their school and learning leadership in the process. After the second year we realized that no one would believe that professional development led by teachers could be so successful, so we approached the Ministry of Education (who controlled the money) and asked that they support us in doing research on TLLP. They concurred and we have done four different studies of the program. We have worked closely with the organizers and, in some ways, are really working together. We provide the data and the evidence, and they have supported the work. Our recommendations based on our research have been taken seriously each time and changes have been made. Maybe we have created yet another type of community that has yielded important research and improved practice, with researchers collaborating with program organizers (Lieberman, Campbell and Yashkina, 2017).

116 A social view of teaching, learning and leading

References

Hargreaves, A. (2010) Change from without: Lessons from other countries, systems, and sectors. In Hargreaves, A., Lieberman, A., Fullan, M., & Hopkins, D. (Eds.), *The Second Handbook of Educational Change*. London: Springer, pp. 105–117.

Lieberman, A., Campbell, C., & Yashkina, A. (2017) *Teacher Learning and Leadership: Of, By, and For Teachers*. London and New York: Routledge.

Lieberman, A. & Wood, D. (2003) *Inside the National Writing Project: Connecting Network Learning and Classroom Teaching*. New York: Teachers College Press.

Sahlberg, P. (2010) Educational change in Finland. In Hargreaves, A., Lieberman, A., Fullan, M., & Hopkins, D. (Eds.), *The Second Handbook of Educational Change*. London: Springer, pp. 323–348.

Talbert, J. (2010) Professional learning communities at the crossroads. In Hargreaves, A., Lieberman, A., Fullan, M., & Hopkins, D. (Eds.), *The Second Handbook of Educational Change*. London: Springer, pp. 555–571.

Weick, K. (1979) *The Social Psychology of Organizing*. Reading, MA: Addison-Wesley Publishers.

Wenger, E. (1998) *Communities of Practice: Learning, Meaning and Identity*. Cambridge: Cambridge University Press

AFTERWORD

When I became a teacher in the 1960s, I never thought that I would become a professor, a writer and a researcher. But clearly part of it was being in the right place at the right time. After several years as a teacher, I needed to get a Masters degree as I clearly knew I needed to learn more about education, kids, schools, leadership and more.

I went to Cal. State Northridge and had some terrific professors. Several of them said I should go and get a doctorate. I had no idea what that would allow me to do, but I liked the idea that the professors I had seemed to do a lot of things – they taught, wrote articles, organized and participated in doing research, gave speeches, and more. This appealed to me as I like to do a lot of things – sometimes at the same time. So I applied to UCLA where I had gotten my undergraduate degree, and got in. And a friend of mine told me to apply for a research position with John Goodlad who had just gotten money to form a school/university partnership (the first of its kind). And I was accepted!

I had already developed a strong passion for representing teachers and teaching. I felt strongly that I had to fight for teacher participation in research studies (about teaching and schooling) and for any ideas that called for teacher improvement so that the complexity of their lives would be represented. I had no idea how to do this, but as this book represents, in part, I was open to learning. When people said to me "maybe you won't get tenure if you take such strong positions about teaching and teachers?", I always replied that I knew I could get a job!

The passion was clearly there, but how could teachers be involved, and how would that change the very nature of research? What did teachers need to know about doing research? Would they be able to articulate a teacher's perspective? How would they learn to *do* research or be partners with researchers? Would I be able to figure out how to have teachers as partners?

Practice makes policy

One thing I learned early on was that if you were going to be in the university, you had to learn to write. And if you were going to represent a teacher's perspective, that would have to be written about as well. I decided that I needed to learn to write about the teacher's work and how it should be considered in any efforts at school improvement (Lieberman, 1982). I started by writing about how policies that mandated change or improvement would fail unless the policymakers understood the social realities of the teacher. And I knew I loved working and writing with others. I liked the discussion, how to think about what to write and where to send our written work!

The conditions for teacher development

I then realized that policies were not the only problematic thing for teachers. What about professional development that was often offered without anyone asking us about the context of our class (our school or our district). We needed to have a variety of conditions that we could describe that were sensitive to the teacher's life. We could describe them as having:

- Norms of collaboration
- Access to a wide range of resources
- A focus on student learning

- Continuous support from the administration
- A reasonable timetable for learning
- Time and help dealing with the challenges

We were all to learn over time that we needed to learn and practice how to organize and understand the five C's:

- Context matters
- Commitments take time to develop
- Capacity of members grows over time
- Content needs balance with process
- Challenges are endemic to any social enterprise

But the ideas for what teachers were to do to improve their work kept shifting over time in important ways. There were professional communities, networks, teacher leaders, partnerships of all kinds, mentors to help newer teachers and more. . . What we saw as teachers was that most professional development had little connection to our classroom problems. Experts who came and provided occasional advice didn't know much about the daily life of a teacher and his or her classroom. And teachers were often asked to participate in improving their teaching as individuals rather than cohorts who could be *supportive* and *helpful* over time. Teacher voices were rarely, if ever, given any prominence in the choices, planning and implementation of improvement efforts. Where was the time to practice new learnings? Did it matter if we were new at teaching, experienced or already expert at our work?

Teachers and school reform

For years, the development of teachers and school reform have been closely linked. They have been characterized by top-down policies and bottom-up participation. There is the "training model" constantly being challenged by the "growth in practice model". Each has to be concerned with the changing realities of teaching practice and how they can lead to improvement with authentic teacher participation.

Professional learning has come to characterize the "growth in practice" model, beginning with Sarason (1971, 1996) where he described the importance of the school culture and its connection to understanding teachers and teaching. And later it was deepened by Shulman (1986) when he characterized "pedagogical content knowledge", which described the complexity of teaching as having not only content knowledge, but how the content connects to teaching. Donald Schön (1983) was the first to focus on reflection and its importance in improving practice. And a little later, Wenger introduced the idea of "communities of practice", focusing attention on those who practice and the importance of building relationships among the people in their work. At the same time, Elmore and McLaughlin (1988) wrote a critical piece advancing the idea that teachers getting better at their work are engaged in what they called *steady work* grounded in the day-to-day realities of classroom life. Moving a step further, Cochran-Smith and Lytle (1999) began to link the idea of teacher development with the development of community. Their distinctions about knowledge *for* practice, *in* practice, and *of* practice helped bring us closer to teachers' working lives.

These were the people who influenced me, as their research work was focusing not just on policies, but on the way in which teachers practiced and thought about their work. They all helped the educational field move closer to the classroom, explaining the structures of reform and the link to the necessary understandings of the complexities of practice.

Starting with teaching practice

It wasn't until Diane Wood and I did research on the National Writing Project (NWP) that I really understood three important ideas about school reform and the involvement of teachers. The first was the power of starting with what teachers knew (their own practice) rather than what researchers knew. The second was the vital importance of creating networks and communities who could both learn new ideas and support each other over time (Lieberman and Grolnick, 1997). I knew about organizations, but was to learn about networks and why they were becoming an important organizational reform. And the third idea was to really understand how professional development could be responsive to what teachers already knew that opened them up to learning from their peers and also from research. Rooted in the NWP's dual commitment to writing-to-learn and teachers teaching other teachers, these activities released both professional knowledge and professional relationships. All these activities stressed learning as a *social* phenomenon (Wenger, 1998). See Chapter 7 for the details of how the NWP created a national phenomenon that is over thirty years old.

Making teaching practice public: Learning in the 21st century

There is now much agreement that the teacher is the key figure in any changes needed in a school (Hatch et al, 2005). But it took a while before there was local, sustainable and economical teacher learning experiences that utilized professional learning communities and incorporated the use of technology. And it has taken much time before there has been an acceptance that teacher knowledge must be made public so that it can be shared, critiqued and verified. New media tools and social networks have begun to promote the idea of *professional knowledge* and the ways in which professional development can be organized. It has taken a long time to move from our understanding of teacher isolation and what it does to your thinking as a teacher (Lortie, 1975) to an understanding of the importance of collegiality (Little, 1982). It was this seminal work that really taught me how teachers who planned and worked together over time not only built commitment to each other, but to their further learning. Even the idea of "struggling" together helped teachers learn new ideas and practices.

From colleagueship to community

It has only been quite recently that several researchers have called for the thinking about professional development to change radically (Cochran-Smith and Lytle, 2009; Lieberman and Miller, 2001). There is now new language and much new evidence talking about what it takes to move the isolation of teachers to professional learning communities (PLCs). The idea of a professional community has collegiality built in, but we are coming to understand how teachers work together, how different communities learn differently, and about how some of the PLCs really stretch what it means to be a teacher and to have access to continuous learning over one's career.

Putting teacher development online: Going public

One of the things we learned was that as teachers talked together and got comfortable talking about their teaching, it was not such a big step to put teaching online as another way of "going public" (see Chapter 6). The documentation of how this began has been done by Desiree Pointer Mace (2009). It was Desiree, who was a member of our team at the Carnegie Foundation for the Advancement of Teaching, who taught us how to do this and how to use the internet to finally get inside teaching, with the teachers showing us what the complexity of teaching looks like when it is publically displayed (see insideteaching.org).

Teachers learning and leading

I never thought that I would see teachers writing proposals, getting money and support, and learning leadership in the process. This is precisely what happened in Toronto, Ontario over ten years ago (Lieberman, Campbell and Yashkina, 2017) when the *Teacher Learning and Leadership* program began (see Chapter 9). It was here that I finally learned that the whole system, including the government as well as the teacher unions, could collaborate on a program that helps to develop teacher knowledge even as it is run by teachers. This program has been going for ten years and is spreading the idea that a system of development for teachers can be successful when it starts with teachers as leaders of their own development (Campbell, Lieberman and Yashkina, 2015).

This was an incredible learning experience for all of us. We knew *why* we needed to have teachers involved in research, but this gave us some much-needed knowledge of *how* it could be organized, led and sustained over time.

References

Campbell, C., Lieberman, A., & Yashkina, A. (2015) Teachers leading educational improvements: Developing teachers' leadership, improving practices and collaboration to share knowledge. *Leading and Managing*, 21(2), 90–105.

Cochran-Smith, M. & Lytle, S. (1999) Teacher learning in communities. *Review of Research in Education*, 24, 249–306.

Cochran-Smith, M. & Lytle, S. (2009) *Inquiry as Stance: Practitioner Research for the Next Generation.* New York: Teachers College Press.

Elmore, R. & McLaughlin, M. (1988) *Steady Work: Policy, Practice and the Reform of American Education.* Santa Monica, CA: Rand Corporation.

Hatch, T., Ahmed, A., Lieberman, A, Faigenbaum, D., White, M.E., & Pointer-Mace, D.H. (2005) *Going Public with Our Teaching: An Anthology of Practice.* New York: Teachers College Press.

Lieberman, A. (1982) Practice makes policy: The tensions of school improvement. In Lieberman, A. & McLaughlin, M. (Eds.), *Policy Making in Education: Eighty-first Yearbook of the National Society for the Study of Education.* Chicago: University of Chicago Press.

Lieberman, A. & Grolnick, M. (1997) Networks, reform and the professional development of teachers. In Hargreaves, A. (Ed.), *Rethinking Educational Change with Heart and Mind.* Alexandria, VA: Association for Supervision and Curriculum Development, pp. 192–215.

Lieberman, A. & Miller, L. (2001) *Teachers Caught in the Action: Professional Development that Matters.* New York: Teachers College Press.

Lieberman, A., Campbell, C., & Yashkina, A. (2017) *Teacher Learning and Leadership: Of, By, and For Teachers.* London and New York: Routledge.

Little, J.W. (1982) Norms of collegiality and experimentation: Workplace conditions of school success. *American Educational Research Journal*, 19(3), 325–340.

Lortie, D. (1975) *Schoolteacher.* Chicago: University of Chicago Press.

Mace, Desiree Pointer (2009) *Teacher Practice Online: Sharing Wisdom, Opening Doors.* New York: Teachers College Press.

Sarason, S. (1971) *The Culture of the School and the Problem of Change.* Boston: Alyn & Bacon

Sarason, S. (1996) *Revisiting "The Culture of the School and the Problem of Change".* New York: Teachers College Press.

Schön, D. (1983) *The Reflective Practitioner.* New York: Basic Books.

Shulman, L. (1986) Those who understand: Knowledge growth in teaching. *Educational Researcher*, 15(2), 4–14.

Wenger, E.(1998) *Communities of Practice: Learning, Meaning, and Identity.* Cambridge: Cambridge University Press.

INDEX

Note: italic page numbers indicate figures.

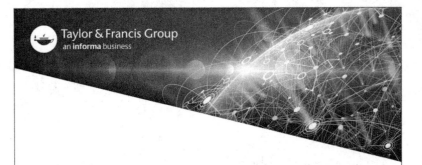